Love 'N' Lactation
Breastfeeding Essentials
Practice • Patience • Persistence

Sekesa Berry,
Midwife & Lactation Consultant

Love 'N' Lactation: Breastfeeding Essentials
Practice • Patience • Persistence

REVISED EDITION
Copyright © August 2022
Published by
Love 'N' Touch, LLC
Hampton, Georgia

All Rights Reserved
All rights reserved. No part of this book may be reproduced, stored in retrieval systems or transmitted in any form or by any means, including mechanical, electronic, photocopying, recording or otherwise, without written permission from the author and or the publisher, except for the use of brief quotation

ISBN 979-8-9854062-1-4

Library of Congress Control Number: - 2021916738

Printed in the United States
Edited by Amunet Berry-Blunt
Cover Art by Sekesa Berry of Love 'N' Touch, LLC
Photo Contribution by Ariel Taylor
Cover photo rights reserved by Love 'N' Touch, LLC

Publisher Contact Information

Love 'N' Touch, LLC
11345 Tara Blvd. Ste 4-279 • Hampton, GA 30228
info@loventouch.com
www.loventouch.com

Love 'N' Lactation

Breastfeeding Essentials

Practice • Patience • Persistence

Table of Contents

Words of Wisdom 1

Why Breastfeed? 6

What is in the milk? 19

Listening to the Experts 29

The Do's & Don'ts of Breastfeeding 35

Five Tips to Breastfeeding Success 48

Solutions to 9 Common Breastfeeding Concerns 66

Dispelling 19 Myths About Breastfeeding 91

Food for Thought 106

Closing Remind-hers 109

About the Author 112

Bibliography 115

Practice • Patience • Persistence

Words of Wisdom

Breastfeeding Essentials

As a woman thinks; so will she be...

When I decided to breastfeed my first child, I quickly realized that my experice would be an independent journey. During my time before social media and Google, we had word of mouth, libraries and, in some fortunate cases, community support. I was the first in at least two generations to commit to breastfeeding. My mother has told me many times that her mother breastfed her briefly. My maternal grandmother birthed eight children, that I'm aware of, and my mother was the only one to *taste her mother's milk*. As a result, all of her daughters (my aunties) bottlefed their babies, and so did all of my female cousins. My father's side was a similar narrative. My paternal grandmother birthed five children, that I'm aware of, and bottlefed all of them. Surprisingly, as a teenager, I witnessed my grandmother's yougest daughter breastfeed both of her children, and for me the seed was planted. From that reference point breastfeeding was normalized in my mind.

I was an idealistic first-time mom at 22 years young. My first wasband and I had come into our own awareness about the world and decided to live and parent our baby as natural as possible. As to be expected, we attempted to birth unmedicated and to breastfeed our son. Unfortuantely, my birth experience was the catalyst for many of the struggles we encountered during our first feeds, the first days and several weeks to come. I recall my labor and being close to delivery when the obstetrician ordered an epidural for me against my wishes. He said "*this has gone on long enough and you won't be able to handle the pain*". What I didn't realize at the time was he meant the pain of an episiotomy and vacuum extraction. The next couple

Practice • Patience • Persistence

of days after birth were very challeging for me to breastfeed. My body, especially my perineum, was terrabliy sore and I felt woozy from all the drugs. Our son was also woozy from the drugs and traumatized from being forcefully extracted by pulling on his little skull, followed by a circumsicion 24 hours postbirth. This discomfort coupled with swollen breasts led to an unbeknowing, inadequate latch that caused painful nipple bruising.

Lactation support in Newport News, Hampton Roads, Virginia, was scarce for me during this time. My family, including my wasband, quickly lost faith in my ability to breastfeed our son. They couldn't understand why I was so determined despite all the pain and a stong-willed infant who was refusing to latch. For me I simply knew within my being that I could do it! I had seen my aunt breastfeed her children sucessfully and I had witnessed other women breastfeed their babies as well. These shining models gave me hope during some very dark moments of self-condemnation. But I soon realized that practice, patience, and persistence were the primary tools needed for me to continue my breastfeeding journey.

Psychodynamics play a crucial role in a woman's breastfeeding experience. The environment and thoughts of a woman have the potential to negatively impact her breastfeeding goals because breastfeeding is more than just a physical act. It deeply involves the emotions and mental state of both the mother and the baby(s). If a mother believes she is not capable of producing milk for her baby, or that she is not producing enough milk, then she will unconsciously increase her cortisol (stress) hormones which interferes with her milk producing hormones; thus, resulting in a decrease in milk supply. In order to obtain a harmonious breastfeeding experience, the mother must remain patient, relaxed, and confident in her body's ability to nourish herself and her baby as it did during pregnancy.

I specialize in helping mothers examine their wholistic (entire) breastfeeding experience. While assessing the physiological challenges that the mother shares with me during a lactation consultation, I am also evaluating her overall emotional well-being. I'm taking her home life into careful consideration and weighing the impact that her day-to-day life is having on her present breastfeeding experience. I consider concerns such as:

- Does the mother have daily postpartum support?
- How well is the mother hydrating, resting, and eating?
- Is the mother preserving any self-time to do activities that she enjoys?
- Are there other young children at home that the mother must tend to during the day?
- What is the husband's/partner's work schedule?
- How well does the father/partner interact with the baby?
- Does the mother have any breastfeeding goals, and if yes what are they?
- What beliefs (if any) are the mother holding related to breastfeeding?

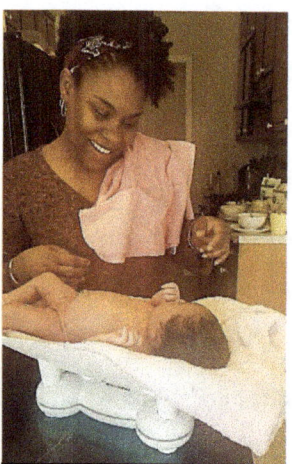

Sekesa weighing a baby post-feed during a routine postpartum home visit.

Practice • Patience • Persistence

- What fears (if any) does the mother have associated with breastfeeding?

All of these concerns are very real to a woman who is also trying to adjust to meeting the growing needs of a new baby. I like to think of myself as not only a Lactation Consultant but also a Breastfeeding **Support Specialist (Doula)** - supporting the wholistic needs of the mother, the father, and the baby to encourage a harmonious breastfeeding experience.

During your breastfeeding journey remember to be kind to yourself. Set realistic goals for each feed. Also remember that though your breastmilk is essential for the growth of your baby, your love, attention, hugs, and kisses are what your baby needs most.

Why Breastfeed?

Economic Impact of Not Breastfeeding

The benefits of breastfeeding for both mom and baby are incredible in terms of health (mentally & physically), economics, and environment. The health benefits will be detailed shortly, however, let us first explore the economic advantages.

Currently in the United States, infant formula has remained one of the most frequently stolen grocery items, which explains why stores keep formula under surveillance and/or lock and key. Even with these protective efforts in place, infant formula continues to be among the top ten shoplifted items nationally, as reported by Organized Retail Theft or ORT. The equation for this ongoing problem is simply: <u>(love + need) poverty = theft</u>.

Formula for Theft Success: Steal Food For a Baby
By Jessica Hopper, ABC News

> <u>Infant formula has become such a hot commodity among sophisticated theft rings that it's been called "liquid gold."</u> The scale of baby formula shoplifting is so vast that it has become an interstate problem, drawn in the FBI and Immigration and Customs Enforcement, and forced chain stores to install elaborate anti-theft devices. Federal legislation has even been introduced that would make stealing baby formula subject to federal racketeering laws. It is a problem on both coasts and hits small stores as well big chains.

The average cost of a regular 16-oz can of branded powder infant formula ranges $15-$20 per can. By two months of age a baby can consume as much as 10 cans of infant formula monthly, costing the parents a rough average of $150-$200/monthly and $1800-$2400 annually.

Unfortunately, if the baby can only digest a specialty infant formula, this amount quickly doubles. Specialty formulas average $25 - $40 per 12oz can, whereas a two-month-young baby will consume approximately 13 cans monthly. This averages a monthly cost of $325 - $520 and an estimated $3,900 - $6,240 annually.

We must also be mindful that on average, Black and Latino American male children tend to have greater sensitivity to cow-milk proteins resulting in this population having a greater need for soy-based or specialty infant formulas.

Babies Fed Soy-based Formula Have Changes in Reproductive System Tissues, CHOP co-author of NIH-led study: subtle estrogen-like responses in infants point to need for longer-term follow-up of effects
Published on Mar 12, 2018 in CHOP News

Some mothers who don't breastfeed have long used soy formula as an alternative to cow-milk formula, often from concerns about milk allergies, lactose intolerance, or other feeding difficulties. However, soy protein contains high amounts of genistein, an estrogen-like compound. <u>Like other estrogen-mimicking chemicals found in the environment, genistein can alter the body's endocrine system and potentially interfere with normal hormonal development.</u>

Lactose Intolerance in Infants, Children, and Adolescents
Melvin B. Heyman and; for the Committee on Nutrition

> ...the prevalence of primary lactase deficiency <u>is 50% to 80% in Hispanic people, 60% to 80% in black</u> and Ashkenazi Jewish people, and almost 100% in Asian and American Indian people.9–11 The age of onset and its prevalence differ among various populations. <u>Approximately 20% of Hispanic, Asian, and black children younger than 5 years of age</u> have evidence of lactase deficiency and lactose malabsorption

The cost of infant formula should be a major influence in a parent's decision to breastfeed. However, there are programs like Women Infant Children (WIC) which was established by the United States Department of Agriculture (USDA) in 1972 to aid in supplementing the overall cost of infant formula. From birth to 3 months, WIC provides about 9 cans of powder formula monthly. By 4 months WIC provides about 10 cans of formula monthly. Many public hospitals and county health departments will have in-house WIC offices for convenient access to families. To this effort, WIC serves as a two-headed dragon. One head promotes health and nutritional programing by providing low-income families with access to specific food items within select brands, such as peanut butter, beans, milk, cereal, and fruit juices. This head also offers breastfeeding support via Peer Counselors and breast pumps. While the other head enforces vaccinations and provides low-grade infant formula, which excuses hundreds of thousands of families from breastfeeding whereby indirectly aiding in infant mortality, childhood diabetes, and maternal breast cancer.

> The Special Supplemental Nutrition Program for Women, Infants, and Children (WIC) provides federal grants to states for supplemental foods, health care referrals, and nutrition education for low-income pregnant, breastfeeding, and non-breastfeeding postpartum women, and to infants and children up to age five who are found to be at nutritional risk.
> fns.usda.gov/wic

Breastfeeding Essentials

Food and Nutrition Service USDA
- WIC at a Glance

>WIC operates through 1,900 local agencies in 10,000 clinic sites, in 50 State health departments, 34 Indian Tribal Organizations, the District of Columbia, and five territories (Northern Mariana, American Samoa, Guam, Puerto Rico, and the Virgin Islands).

I worked as a WIC Breastfeeding Peer Counselor for my local health department in Clayton County, GA for over three years, and my department promoted breastfeeding consistently. We, as a team of four women, implemented mandatory breastfeeding classes for every pregnant woman and offered breast pump incentives to exclusively breastfeeding families. We were responsible for case management for breastfeeding families, and we even offered a monthly breastfeeding support group. My best statistical average was for every class of 20 women, ten would initiate (put baby to breast after birth) breastfeeding. Of that ten, one possibly would exclusively breastfeed for six months or longer. Most of these women fell to the temptation of free formula, much like the epidural offered in hospitals during childbirth.

Ultimately, in the United States, the cost of infant formula is a less significant barrier due to programs like WIC and Food Stamps. Most low-income families use these programs to off-set the cost of infant formula. Typically, the middle to upper income families are taxed with the pinch of paying cash for infant formula. Coincidently, these are also the same communities where breastfeeding has greater initiation and duration.

Environmental Impact of Not Breastfeeding

Breastfeeding is considered the most environmentally friendly food for all mammals. It generates zero waste, zero greenhouse gases, and has no water footprint. Breast milk essentially does not require farming, packaging, shipping, storage, or heating. Zero prep time is required! It is ready to use immediately from the source.

On the contrary, when we consider the milk alternative, infant formula, it has an astounding environmental impact and a heavy carbon footprint. It has been noted as an *unsustainable global feeding method*.

No One Is Talking About The Environmental Impacts of The Baby Formula Industry. Carly Cassella, 17 July 2018

> Now consider the alternative: formula milk requires farming, storage, pasteurization, drying, cooling, packaging, and shipping. Experts say that every kilogram of powdered infant milk requires roughly 4,000 liters of water.
>
> Not to mention the fact that powdered milk comes from cows, <u>and the cattle industry is the second largest contributor to methane emissions</u> - a heat trapping gas around 30 times more potent than CO_2.

When we observe the production pathway of infant formula, it becomes apparent as to why this method of infant feeding is globally unsustainable. Let us begin with the dairy cow. A farm raised dairy cow requires over 20 pounds of cattle feed plus supplements and water daily to produce milk. Many dairy farmers will mix recycled candy such as jellybeans, chocolate bars and gummy candies into their cattle feed to offset the cost of corn and to make the milk sweeter.

Cattle farmers struggling with record corn prices are feeding their cows candy instead.
- CNN Money, New York

>That's right, candy. Cows are being fed chocolate bars, gummy worms, ice cream sprinkles, marshmallows, bits of hard candy and even powdered hot chocolate mix, according to cattle farmers, bovine nutritionists, and commodities dealers.
>
>"It has been a practice going on for decades and is a very good way for producers to reduce feed cost, and to provide less expensive food for consumers," said Ki Fanning, a livestock nutritionist with Great Plains Livestock Consulting, Inc. in Eagle, Neb.

Once the cow produces the milk then it is removed via a pumping system, blended with numerous other cow's milk, and stored (waiting for pasteurization). After pasteurization, the milk is further processed to separate 2%, low fat, whole milk, powdered milk, etc. The powdered milk is most commonly used by infant formula companies as a primary ingredient in the formula. These companies blend the powdered milk with about 20 - 30 other ingredients, then package and ship it to the retailers. All of these methods require some energy source to operate, such as electricity, gas and/or water. Once received by the retailer, the infant formula is then sold to the consumer who adds water (purified) to it, shakes it well, and feeds it to their baby. Even the ready to feed formula brands require similar preparations before shipping.

Practice • Patience • Persistence

> **INGREDIENTS:** 35.5% CORN MALTODEXTRIN, 17.5% CASEIN HYDROLYSATE (DERIVED FROM MILK), 14.5% SUGAR (SUCROSE), 9.7% HIGH OLEIC SAFFLOWER OIL, 9.5% MEDIUM CHAIN TRIGLYCERIDES, 8.0% SOY OIL; **LESS THAN 2% OF:** C. COHNII OIL*, M. ALPINA OIL†, CALCIUM PHOSPHATE, DATEM, POTASSIUM CITRATE, XANTHAN GUM, MAGNESIUM CHLORIDE, MONOGLYCERIDES, SODIUM CHLORIDE, ASCORBIC ACID, L-CYSTINE DIHYDROCHLORIDE, CALCIUM CARBONATE, L-TYROSINE, POTASSIUM CHLORIDE, CHOLINE CHLORIDE, FERROUS SULFATE, L-TRYPTOPHAN, TAURINE, m-INOSITOL, ASCORBYL PALMITATE, dl-ALPHA-TOCOPHERYL ACETATE, ZINC SULFATE, L-CARNITINE, NIACINAMIDE, MIXED TOCOPHEROLS, CALCIUM PANTOTHENATE, CUPRIC SULFATE, VITAMIN A PALMITATE, THIAMINE CHLORIDE HYDROCHLORIDE, RIBOFLAVIN, PYRIDOXINE HYDROCHLORIDE, FOLIC ACID, POTASSIUM IODIDE, POTASSIUM HYDROXIDE, PHYLLOQUINONE, BIOTIN, SODIUM SELENATE, VITAMIN D_3, AND CYANOCOBALAMIN.

-Similac baby formula ingredient list

There is ongoing, seemingly dismissive, conversations between developed and industrialized countries regarding greenhouse gasses, global warming, fresh water, and carbon footprints. These terms in short describe the negative impacts that we as huemans are having on our planet with machinery, technology, and unsustainable lifestyle practices. Our reckless behavior with industrialization is causing long-lasting and, in some cases, irreversible effects to our environment in terms of the quality of air we breathe, the foods we eat and the drinkable water we need to live. We are poisoning the air with CO_2 emissions from automobiles, factories, and farms; over- heating our atmosphere with radiation and microwaves; contaminating and over-using our freshwater reserves; deforesting the land; killing the animals; and genetically altering the foods. The environmental issues we are facing extend well beyond breastfeeding; however, the lack thereof is a direct reflection of huemanity's blatant disregard for nature, or our interest in being a symbiotic part of the greater spectrum of life on this planet. We truly are living an unsustainable reality!

Risks to Non-Breastfeeding Mother

The breastfeeding benefits for both mom and baby are vast and astonishing. When we, as huemans, behave in accordance with nature's design, then we are privy to certain biological benefits or health gains. On the contrary, when we operate against this design then we tend to forfeit those same benefits and potentially suffer. An example of this is artificially straightening or perming of the hair. We are the only species on this planet that alter our hair/fur and as a result many people suffer wholistically with headaches, bad skin, scalp infections, balding, hormonal imbalance, fibroids, tumors, and even cancer.

Permanent Hair Dyes, Straighteners Linked to Higher Breast Cancer Risk
-Breastcancer.org December 9, 2019

Research suggests that nearly 75% of Black women use some type of chemical relaxer/straightener on their hair.

Research also shows that hair products contain more than 5,000 chemicals, including some considered to be hormone disrupters. Hormone disruptors can affect how estrogen and other hormones act in the body, by blocking them or mimicking them, which throws off the body's hormonal balance. Because estrogen can make hormone-receptor-positive breast cancer develop and grow, many women choose to limit their exposure to these chemicals that can act like estrogen. Other chemicals that make up hair dye have been found to cause mammary gland tumors in rats.

Practice • Patience • Persistence

Chemical treatments used to permanently or semi-permanently straighten or relax hair also contain a mixture of chemicals. Many straighteners contain formaldehyde, which is considered a carcinogen, a substance capable of causing cancer.

Likewise with breastfeeding, when we decide to stop a naturally occurring process like lactation by binding our breasts or taking supplements to discourage the milk supply, then our bodies suffer wholistically. According to the National Center for Biotechnology Information (NCBI), "**non-breastfeeding mothers are at higher risks** *of breast cancer and ovarian cancer, as well as obesity, type 2 diabetes, metabolic syndrome, and cardiovascular disease.*" There is also greater potential for both postpartum hemorrhage and postpartum depression. Ultimately, continuing a naturally occurring biological process, such as breastfeeding your baby, grants biological protections from several of the aforementioned ailments.

There are also other immeasurable benefits to the breastfeeding mother such as feeling more empowered, confident, and proud.

We are all energetically and cosmically connected. I am my sister's keeper, and our community is only as strong as our weakest link. This truth is evident within the breakdown and disconnect of our communities. Breastfeeding bonds the child to the mother who should be bonded to her community. In turn as the child grows then they too will be bonded to their community. This bond creates kinship and extended family, whereas my child is your child. This relationship has been greatly disrupted with the intentional displacement of breastfeeding.

Risks to Non-Breastfed Baby

What we claim as benefits to breastfeeding a baby truly are normal biological processes granted when we are compliant with nature's design. It is only when we seize to comply with this demand that we face disparities. Similar to the mother, there can be grave consequences for the baby by not breastfeeding and exclusively using infant formula. The National Center for Biotechnological Information (NCBI) reports, *"for infants, not being breastfed is associated with an increased incidence of infectious morbidity, as well as elevated risks of childhood obesity, type 1 and type 2 diabetes, leukemia, and sudden infant death syndrome."* There is also greater risk of digestive issues such as constipation, colic, reflux, respiratory issues like asthma and allergies, skin irritations such as eczema and infant acne, and slower brain development.

Milk formula are a combination of many industrially manufactured ingredients like milk powder, vegetable oil, high fructose corn syrup, sucrose and micronutrients etc. Standard milk formula is a product based on milk of cows or other animals and/or other ingredients, which have been generally agreed to be suitable for infant feeding, though its inadequacies as an alternative to breastfeeding are well established , .Also, powdered infant formula is not a sterile product even if it has been manufactured to meet current hygiene standards, Cronobacter sakazakii and Salmonella enterica being the pathogens of most concern.

**Carbon Footprints Due to Milk Formula.
A study from selected countries of the Asia Pacific region**

Again, when we allow a naturally occurring process to continue, we reap the benefits. This in no way implies that if a mother chooses to exclusively breastfeed that she and her baby will completely avoid the above-mentioned ailments. There are other biological, environmental, and dietary factors involved. However, the takeaway message here is that **exclusive breastfeeding minimizes the risks** and grants specific protections to both mother and baby.

It is most imperative that Black Americans return to breastfeeding. In the United States, Black Americans have the highest rate of infant loss, SIDS, childhood asthma, diabetes, and depression. These disparities can carry on into adulthood and morph into other diseases.

When evaluating our health disparities in comparison to other racial groups, it becomes clear that we are being (self) eliminated through disease and other measures. Breastfeeding has been an intricate part of Black culture for centuries, and I would argue that this innate and natural act has directly helped us survive continued attack and oppression in this country. To this truth it is necessary that Black Americans return to breastfeeding to help secure our sustainable reality in this country.

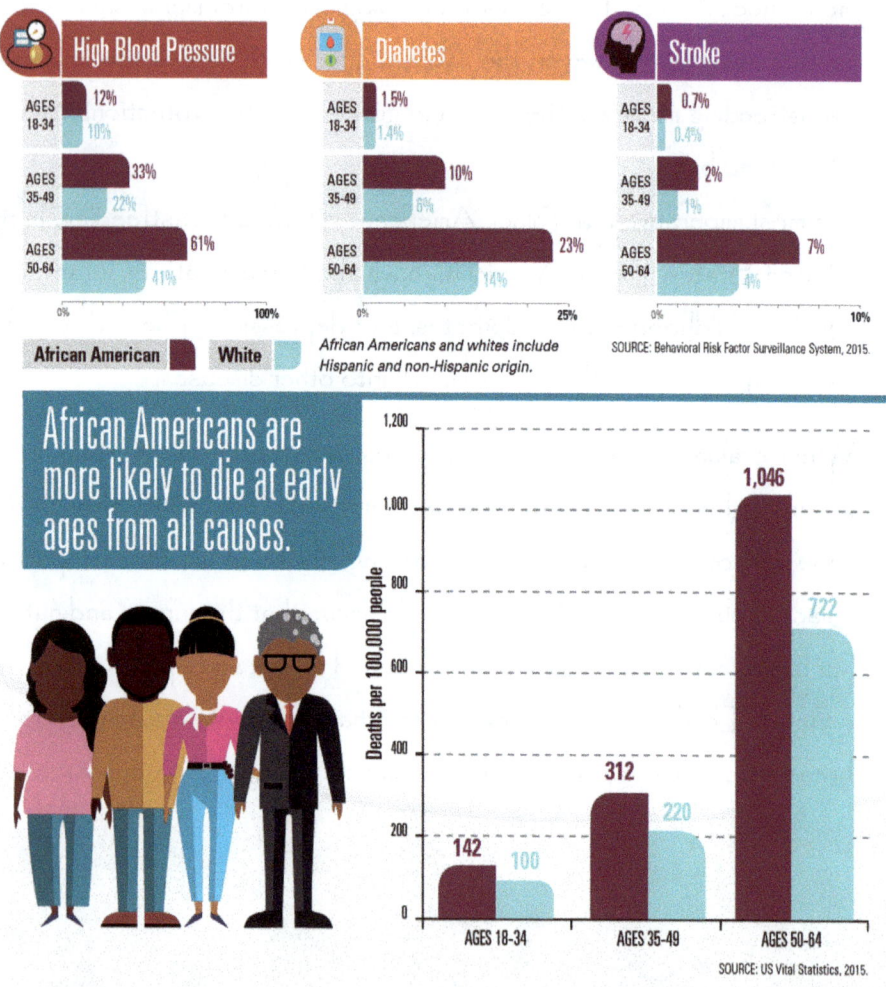

Practice • Patience • Persistence

What's in the Milk?

Breastfeeding Essentials

Have you ever wondered what makes breast milk so great? Considering the appearance of modern science being capable of improving our hueman imperfections through stem cell reconstruction, cloning, genetic modification, and manipulation, how is it that still, today, in 2022 that breast milk composition continues to be superior to science-lab constructed infant formula?

I will not pretend to have all of the answers, but what I do know is that hueman milk is a living, changing, organic, superfood. It is always complete and nutritionally sound to provide for your baby's wholistic needs.

Hueman Breast milk

- Rich in brain-building omega 3s, namely DHA (docosahexaenoic acid) and AA (Arachidonic acid).
- Rich in brain and body building protein components.
- Contains sleep-inducing proteins.
- Rich in oligosaccharides, which promote intestinal health.
- Rich in living white blood cells, millions per feeding.

Breast Milk vs. Formula
- Dr. Sears

    Antibacterial! Antifungal! Antiseptic: Antimicrobial!

National Center for Biotechnology Information
Human Milk Composition: Nutrients and Bioactive Factors

    The composition of human milk is the biologic norm for infant nutrition. <u>Human milk also contains many hundreds to thousands of distinct bioactive molecules that protect against infection and inflammation and contribute to immune maturation, organ development, and healthy</u>

<u>microbial colonization</u>. Some of these molecules, e.g., lactoferrin, are being investigated as novel therapeutic agents.

All mammals lactate and feed milk to their young. This is the purpose of the mammary glands, also known as breasts or teat. This biological process ensures the optimal growth and development of that species. Mammalian milk is species specific and changes over time to meet the needs of that offspring as it grows. It differs in warmer climates to provide more water for hydration vs. more fat in colder climates to provide more girth. Within the milk are the perfect balance of proteins and fats, vitamins and minerals, hormones and enzymes, water, and calories. Mammalian milk also provides a sophisticated combination of antivirals, antibacterials, and antiparasitics. This combination of antibodies works diligently to enhance the lymphatic system (immune system) of the offspring in effort to protect it from any number of worldly pathogens and diseases.

Hueman breast milk contains high amounts of lactose and requires water for production which is why water is abundant in breast milk. The amount of water in breast milk fluctuates throughout the day but maintains an average of about 70%. Hence there is no need to give an exclusively breastfed baby any additional water until the baby is ready for solid foods. An increase of water intake for a breastfeeding mother has been proven to increase her breast milk production.

DNA (Deoxyribonucleic acid) and RNA (ribonucleic acid,) can also be found in mammalian milk. There are at least 146 known genes that are activated with hueman milk that help to protect the infant's digestive system and improve their lymphatic system (immune system).

Breastfeeding Essentials

Breast Milk Does DNA Good
-Robin Nixon May 22, 2010, LiveScience

Researchers have shown that an infant's first food affects his or her gene expression, giving a possible mechanism for how breast milk impacts health. (Gene expression is the process by which instructions in a gene are used to synthesize a functional gene product, mostly proteins. When genes are expressed, it is as if they are "turned on.")

"Genes are really sensitive to nutrition," said study researcher Sharon Donovan of the University of Illinois. "And we now have genes that may explain many of the clinical observations of how breast-fed and formula-fed infants differ."

Using a novel noninvasive technique, researchers compared 10 formula-fed 3-month-olds with 12 breast-fed infants of the same age. Capitalizing on the natural sloughing off of intestinal cells during digestion, the researchers looked for signs of gene expression, in the form of messenger RNA, in the babies' poop.

Breast milk and formula have different effects on at least 146 genes, the researchers found.

Most of the genes enhanced by breast milk promote quick development of the intestine and immune system, Donovan told LiveScience.

"At birth, the poor baby comes out of a nice, protected environment, where everything is taken care of," Donovan said, into a world teeming with bacteria and where nutrition must be obtained from a rookie intestine. The faster the baby's digestion tract and immune system get up to speed, the healthier the child.

Some of the genes positively affected by breast milk protect against "leaky gut," a disorder in which foreign particles enter the bloodstream through the intestinal wall, Donovan said. Leaky gut is thought to increase the risk of allergies and inflammatory diseases, such as asthma, colitis, and Crohn's disease — all of which may have higher rates among formula-fed babies, previous research has suggested.

Breast milk and formula likely affect gene expression in one of two ways, Donovan said. They could change the factors responsible for decoding DNA into its active forms. Or they could have an epigenetic effect, where the DNA spiral is refolded, making certain genes more or less available for use.

The latter (epigenetics) is usually, but not always, permanent and, if this is the mechanism used, it might explain why <u>breast milk can have life-long health benefits</u>.

"Breastmilk evolved to feed human infants, and it contains a number of bioactive elements," Donovan said, such as hormones, growth factors and plentiful fibers.

"Cow's milk (the primary ingredient in formula) evolved to feed calves," Donovan continued. Its composition is much different than human milk, and its bioactive elements are often destroyed during processing, she said.

Of course, manufacturers are continuously trying to tweak formula to make it more like breast milk. "But even though people have been breastfeeding infants for thousands of years," Donovan said, "we [scientists] still have a lot to learn."

Infant Formula simply cannot measure up to Hueman Milk. Infant formula was actually created in 1865 as a desperate attempt to address infant mortality among American and European Whites – notoriety attributed to chemist Justus von Liebig. During that time, it was stated repetitively that infant formula was to be used as an "**emergency food only**" and was not to replace breastfeeding.

Infant Foods | Milk Formulas
-D. Hileti-Telfer, in Encyclopedia of Food Sciences and Nutrition (Second Edition), 2003.

> "Infant formula was designed for use as a substitute for human milk when mothers are unable to breast feed their babies."

I am a firm believer in the saying, "each one teaches one" and "when you know better, you do better." Therefore, as we continue to learn the amazing effects of hueman milk within hueman babies, then it inherently becomes our responsibility to make better choices for ourselves and encourage our sisters and brothers to do the same.

> The use of artificial formula was associated with many summertime infant deaths due to the spoilage of milk left in bottles. This association was not understood, however, until the public accepted germ theory. Between 1890 and 1910, emphasis was placed on cleanliness and the improvement in the quality of milk supplies. Improvements included providing better care for dairy cattle and forming infant milk clinics to disburse clean milk to the public.
> **A History of Infant Feeding, NCBI**

How is the Milk Made?

Breast milk presents in a continuum of three known stages noted as colostrum, transitional milk, and mature milk. Though girls develop breasts during puberty the milk ducts and glands are still immature until she meets a pregnancy halfway; approximately 20 weeks. At this point the body begins

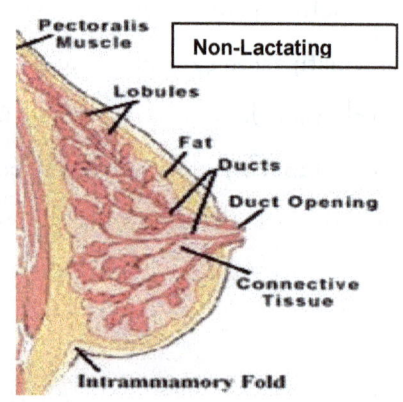

Practice • Patience • Persistence

producing a powerful milk substance called *colostrum*. Some women will begin producing colostrum as early as 16 weeks of pregnancy. It presents as whitish-looking dried solid deposits at the nipples.

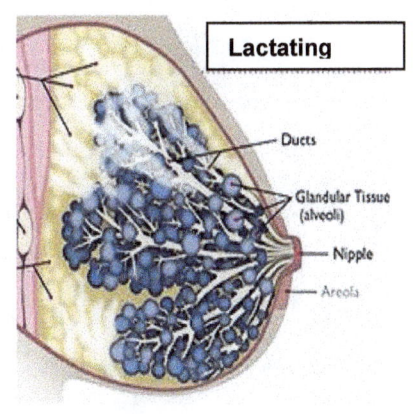

Some women may even experience leaking drops of clear-looking fluid from the nipples. Some women do not see colostrum until birth. All are normal variations, and neither can determine how much milk the woman will make, nor does it reveal a woman's ability to produce milk.

Colostrum is produced in very small amounts and serves as the first infant food. This is critically important since the newborn has never had any food substance in their digestive system. They have only swallowed amniotic fluid. Colostrum is thicker than mature milk due to the less water content. It is a dense and concentrated milk, making every drop nutrient rich. This denseness also makes it difficult to pump. Colostrum appears yellowish orange in color due to the large amounts of beta carotene which works as a powerful antioxidant to help enhance the infant's lymphatic system (immune system). Colostrum is also loaded with antibiotics, making it the infant's first booster shot to help prepare them for this environment. It has high concentrations of sodium, potassium, and chloride which encourage optimal development of the infant's heart, brain, and central nervous system. It is high in protein and fat-soluble vitamins such as Vitamin A & E, which help to regulate the infant's blood sugar. Colostrum has a mild

Breastfeeding Essentials

laxative effect on the newborn to encourage their first bowel movements, called meconium. Meconium is a thick, sticky, dark greenish stool that lines the infant intestinal tract and prevents them from pooping in-utero. The infant must expel this stool within the first 48 hours of birth to help prevent *jaundice**.

About 72 hours after birth the breast milk begins to slowly integrate with mature milk. This integration is referred to as *transitional milk*. At this point the breasts begin to feel and look fuller. Many women experience *engorgement* during this time, specifically if there are challenges with breastfeeding. Transitional milk is stimulated by the detachment of the placenta. Once the placenta detaches there is a biological response and shift of hormones that trigger the second stage of lactation. This stage of lactation persists regardless of a woman's decision to breastfeed. It doesn't require nipple stimulation for production as it is hormonally driven. It is readily available, usually in abundance, as nature's gift and a fail-safe to both mom and baby while breastfeeding is being established.

Transitional milk contains more water, fat, calories, and lactose (natural sugar) than colostrum, however the levels of proteins and immune properties are decreased.

> Colostrum is a living fluid, resembling blood in its composition. It contains over 60 components, 30 of which are exclusive to hueman milk. It is species-specific, designed for hueman babies (Neville and Neifert, 1985).

This gradual shift of milk properties from colostrum to mature milk varies greatly and can range from 7-14 days. This shift can be noted by the color of the breast milk. As the milk matures the color transitions from yellowish white tint to white with light bluish tint.

Mature milk is the term used to describe the final stage of lactation and milk production. This milk can present as early as 10 days postpartum and as late as 20 days. By 3-4 weeks postpartum, your milk is assumed to be completely mature and not contain any colostrum. However, it is still rich in protein, lactose, vitamins, minerals, and an abundance of bioactive ingredients – such as antibiotics, essential growth hormones, and enzymes.

Mature milk will maintain a fundamental consistency of ingredients the entire duration of continued breastfeeding. However, the taste, smell and color can be affected by what you eat (See Chapter 5 Do's and Don'ts of Breastfeeding). Also, the amount of milk you produce can be affected by your lifestyle and the consistency of your breasts being stimulated via pump or baby.

As the milk transitions so does the baby's poop. Remember what goes in must come out. The newborn's stool begins as a dark, thick tarry looking substance called meconium. As the milk transitions a few days after birth, the baby's stool looks more greenish. By one week postpartum the stool will look yellow and seedy (see pictures).

Breastfeeding Essentials

The baby's poop should change color from black to yellow during the first 5 days after birth.

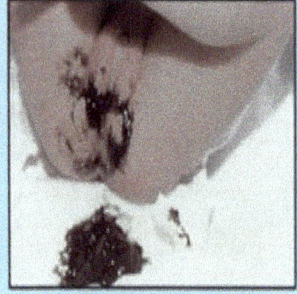

The baby's first poop is black and sticky.

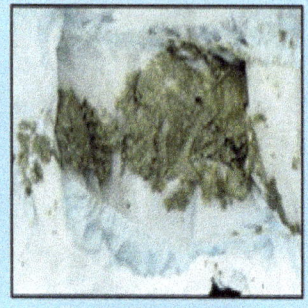

The poop turns green by Day 3 or 4.

The poop should turn yellow by Day 4 or 5.

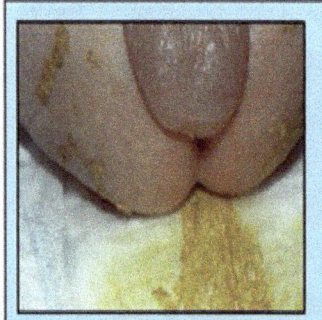

Poop can look seedy.

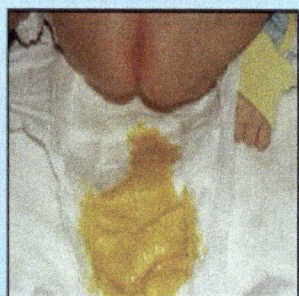

Poop can look watery.

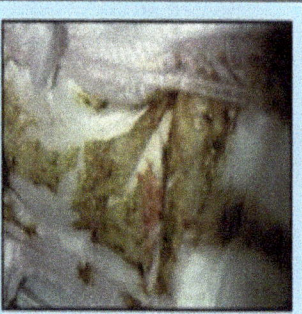

Illness, injury, or allergies can cause blood in poop. Call Doctor.

© 2002 K. Hoover/B. Wilson-Clay Created By Kay Hoover, M Ed, IBCLC and Barbara Wilson-Clay, BS, IBCLC

Practice • Patience • Persistence

Listening to Experts

Expert Overload:

A mother came to my practice with a 10-day young baby. She was overwhelmed with doubts and concerns about her ability to breastfeed and was strongly considering supplementing with some infant formula. Her pediatrician had informed her that the baby had not gained adequate weight and encouraged her to use 2-3 bottles of formula daily. After I spoke with the mom and listened to her birth story, I learned that she had an eventful birth. She had opted for water birth with the vision of blissful birthing and catching her own baby. Instead, she labored in the hospital for two days, where she received Pitocin, fentanyl, antibiotics, and eventually an epidural. She was confined to the bed attached to a fetal heart rate monitor, a contraction monitor, a blood pressure cuff, and a urine catheter. Her baby was eventually delivered with the aid of vacuum extraction. Her baby boy was birthed healthy at 8lb 3 oz, yet by the end of day one there was concerns about his glucose levels and his blood work also revealed early onset of jaundice. The mom felt pressured by the nursing staff to produce milk for her baby. They loaned her a breast pump, but her body was naturally only producing colostrum which is difficult to pump. She tried hand expression but was not very successful. Eventually on day two the neonatal nurses convinced the parents that baby had to have some formula to stabilize his glucose and encourage a bowel movement which would help his jaundice.

Both mom and baby went home on day three and mom was beginning to feel her transitional milk coming in. Her attempts at breastfeeding now were painful but she steadfast and persisted with nursing her baby. These repetitive painful latches damaged her nipples, creating cracks and bruises. By day six the mother

Practice • Patience • Persistence

began to pump her milk and feed it to baby with the bottle. By day eight the pediatrician said the baby was 7lb 12oz and needed to gain more weight. She was very reluctant to use infant formula which is why she scheduled a visit with me.

I weighed the baby at 7lb 14oz, which just so happened to be his weight at discharge from the hospital, and during the oral exam I discovered that he had a mild shallow gag reflex. Before I could address the feeding issues, I first had to help this mother restore her confidence. I had to listen to her story and validate her experience of a failed birth plan. I had to allow her to share her frustrations about feeling like a failure at both birth and now breastfeeding disappointments. After listening to this mama, I then praised her efforts and attempts to be the best mother she knows how to be. I confirmed her challenges of birthing in a hospital with all the interruptions and interventions. The task of consistently answering questions and being bombarded with new information when all you really want to do is hold your baby and sleep. I informed her that these same interruptions could have very likely been the cause of baby's glucose and jaundice issues, as baby truly needed to simply be held by her and not taken away soon after birth to a room filled with strangers.

I then explained the difference between "birth weight" being inflated numbers due to swelling from baby being submerged in water since conception, and "discharge weight" reflecting a more accurate number after some of the swelling has resolved. This revealed that her baby was gaining nicely considering the expectation of baby needing to meet his birth weight by two *weeks of age. The visit continued with correcting his latch and encouraging oral exercises.*

At her one-week follow-up appointment baby weighed 8lb 2oz and was exclusively breastfeeding.

In my service I have noticed that parents, specifically first-time parents, tend to lose their voices and their power throughout their pregnancy and birth. Their knowledge and skills are consistently being challenged by their community and medical providers. They are overwhelmed with advice, risks factors, new terminology, and techniques, as well as a plethora of infant gear & gadgets. These societal attacks can have grave consequences to the confidence and intuition of the parents who will ultimately be the primary care providers to this new baby. It is imperative that the parents remember that they are the experts for their baby. Much information can be gained by asking a breastfeeding mother "*what do you think is the problem.*"

During pregnancy and breastfeeding a family bond is created, specifically between mother and baby. This bond is strengthened by the hormone oxytocin. When a woman births unmedicated, both she and baby will experience high levels of oxytocin immediately after the baby is born. If the father is present, then he too will experience this oxytocin spike. During breastfeeding the mother also releases great amounts of oxytocin, which is necessary for milk ejection. These biochemical responses are necessary for mammals to ensure that we bond and not abandon our offspring.

Pregnancy and breastfeeding also unifies the biorhythms between the mother and her baby. The baby can sense the mother's feelings via electromagnetic energy as well as hormonal chemistry. Thoughts and feelings trigger hormonal releases in our bodies. When we are feeling good and happy, our body's release endorphins such as oxytocin, relaxin, and serotonin. When we are feeling sad, scared, or angry, our body's release stress hormones like cortisol, norepinephrine, and adrenaline. The mom in the story of *Expert Overload*, was feeling stressed and unsure about her abilities to provide for her baby. This mindset caused disharmony between her and the baby as she was relating these feelings biochemically and rhythmically to her baby. By helping to validate her experience and reassuring her role as the primary care provider, she was able to restore her confidence, rebuild her trust in her body and reconnect with her baby, resulting in breastfeeding success.

The American Academy of Pediatrics policy on breastfeeding and use of human milk:

> "Recommendation of exclusive breastfeeding for about 6 months, followed by continued breast- feeding as complementary foods are introduced, with continuation of breastfeeding for 1 year or longer as mutually desired by mother and infant."

With the AAP recommendation I find that many families are aware of, "*exclusive breastfeeding for about 6 months*" section of the statement but are not informed about the "**with continuation of breastfeeding for 1 year or longer**" segment of this statement. Hence the standard breastfeeding goal among Americans has become six months. This is unfortunate for the infant's lymphatic system (immune system) which is said to not be fully developed until onset of puberty.

Breastfeeding Essentials

The World Health Organization recognizes the lymphatic/immune system developmental process and has adopted a policy that better meets this need and gives the infant greater ability to thrive, specifically in rural and underdeveloped areas.

The World Health Organization Breastfeeding Recommendation

> Exclusive breastfeeding is recommended up to 6 months of age, with continued breastfeeding along with appropriate complementary foods <u>up to two years of age or beyond.</u>

There is sound research available that supports extended breastfeeding well beyond the toddler phase and into preschool age. Ultimately, the decision for the duration of breastfeeding your baby resides with the mother and the baby. Some little ones will self-wean before the first year – then there are those who will comfort nurse up to six years. The key phrase promoted by the AAP is for as long "as mutually desired by mother and infant." So feed your baby comfortably and confidently despite the haters and nay-sayers! As the expert of your family, you know what is best for both you and your baby.

Practice • Patience • Persistence

The Do's and Don'ts of Breastfeeding

Breastfeeding Essentials

During pregnancy, many women believe in the myth that they are eating for two. This idea can directly cause women to overeat, resulting in gestational diabetes, pregnancy induced hypertension, and several other pregnancy related conditions. As a lactation consultant, I find that families tend to be more concerned about what the mom consumes while breastfeeding than while pregnant. This is unfortunate, as a mother's diet during pregnancy directly affects the growth and development of her baby. Even her thoughts have great potential to impact the baby due to the biochemical response described in Chapter 4. If a woman is releasing great amounts of stress-related hormones in pregnancy, the baby is more likely to be whiney and clingy. On the contrary, when a woman releases more endorphins, her baby tends to be more secure, content, and happy.

There are many myths surrounding what a breastfeeding mother should and shouldn't consume, in fear of causing harm to either her baby or her milk supply. Myths such as a breastfeeding mother shouldn't eat beans, sweets, or spicy foods; she shouldn't drink alcohol, sodas, or coffee. These concerns can discourage women from breastfeeding.

Unlike pregnancy, breastfeeding grants more deviation from an otherwise healthy diet and does not impact the health of baby. Breast milk production involves a more elaborate filtration process. Whereby fewer toxins and waste materials reach the baby's bloodstream. On the contrary, a continuous unhealthy diet will eventually impact the mother's health.

Alcohol, for example, when consumed in excess during pregnancy can cause fetal growth restrictions and poor brain development. While excessive alcohol consumption during breastfeeding can lead to mom having mastitis and low milk production, the milk will still fundamentally be the same quality.

What we now know about breast milk production is, though it is derived directly from the mother's blood supply, the pathway by which the milk is both formed and delivered to the baby's bloodstream is armed with filters. It begins in the mother's mouth. Here food/beverages are meshed with her saliva, containing enzymes that initiate the break down process. As the food continues through the mom's digestive system it will meet numerous enzymes and filters that extract insoluble food particles, waste, and harmful materials in effort to absorb viable nutrients. These nutrients enter the mom's bloodstream and are used to maintain her health and to make breast milk. Once the milk enters the baby's mouth, it must continue a similar break down process before being absorbed into the baby's bloodstream. This intricate pathway greatly limits the amount of waste and toxins that enters the milk and increases the concentration of nutrients.

With this knowledge, much breast milk research has been explored to determine the concentration and effects of food and beverage items, as well as pharmaceuticals. The results directly debunk many common food myths associated with breastfeeding. For example, it is widely believed that garlic consumption can make babies gassy and fussy, however a controlled study involving breastfeeding mothers chosen to ingest a supplement of garlic before nursing revealed that their babies actually had longer than average feeds with no signs of digestive discontent afterwards. Babies in the garlic supplement group actually fed 20% longer and consumed more milk, indicating a preference for the taste of garlic.

Most foods are allowed during breastfeeding and cause little to no effects in the milk or in the baby. A breastfeeding mother is encouraged to eat similarly as she did during pregnancy. **Be aware that if a breastfeeding mother has a sensitivity to a specific food item causing her indigestion, then it can potentially cause digestive issues in her baby as well.** Listed below are some signs to alert you that your baby is having digestive issues, in which case consult a lactation specialist:

- Fussiness and/or inconsolable crying for long lengths of time
- Disturbed sleep cycle with inconsolable crying
- Consistent: diarrhea, green stools, mucousy stool, or vomiting
- Baby acne, eczema, hives, rash
- Wheezing and/or coughing

FOODS ALLOWED that were once discouraged

Cow's milk	Eggs	Broccoli
Cabbage	Beans	Sweet potatoes
Garlic	Onions	Ginger
Turmeric	Cinnamon	Other Spices

Junk food such as, potato chips, cookies, cake, ice cream, candy, etc. should be eaten in moderation. Though these foods do not degrade the breast milk, they can negatively impact the mother's health when consumed frequently. If you are eating crappy, low-quality food then you will feel crappy or fatigued and may be discouraged from breastfeeding.

Prenatal Vitamins are encouraged during breastfeeding; however, consult your healthcare provider or nutritionist before consuming any new vitamin and/or supplements. Always choose plant-based supplements as they are more easily digested and absorbed into the body.

Foods allowed in Moderation

Spicy Foods – Strong spices can leech into the taste of breast milk, particularly when used in abundance. Some babies love spicy flavors, whereas others do not. Too much spicy foods such as cayenne, jalapeño, scotch bonnet, habanero, ghost pepper and the likes can irritate baby's mouth and/or cause digestive irritation. For this reason, be mindful of your consumption of these foods and be aware of baby's behavior after breastfeeding.

Caffeine – Caffeine sensitivity can vary from one person to the next, so be mindful of your daily consumption. Excessive amounts of caffeine found in coffee and colas can cause a decrease in milk supply. Be mindful of hidden caffeine as well, such as in dark chocolate, green and black tea, and energy drinks.

Herbs – Since everyone responds to herbs differently, they should always be consumed to bowel tolerance. Due diligence in researching an herb before consumption is a must as most herbs are not FDA approved

Breastfeeding Essentials

or tested. Certain herbs such as those listed below are believed to cause a decrease in milk supply. However, remember there is little to no threat when used moderately as seasoning, garnish, or as a single cup of tea.

Sage	Black Walnut	Chickweed
Peppermint	Spearmint	Lemon Balm
Stinging Nettles	Oregano	Parsley

Cannabis – With the rapid legalization of cannabis, even for medical use, it is important to know the facts. Cannabis, in any form, should only be consumed in strict moderation. Unfortunately, due to legal restrictions in most states, this limits access to quality cannabis, whereas a breastfeeding mother would be privy to choose the appropriate strand that would deliver specific effects. There are over 700 known strands of cannabis and limited research to determine the direct effects in breast milk or infant behavior. There are anecdotal studies where mothers claim to have a greater milk supply after eating cannabis. However, we cannot conclude the strain or dosage she used to render those results. Nonetheless, what we can conclude is certain strands of cannabis do affect mental perception which can lead to irresponsible parental behavior. It also must be noted that some street cannabis can be laced with other drugs such as codeine-based cough syrup or embalming fluid, PCP, fentanyl, heroin, cocaine, and/or LSD. So, if you choose to use cannabis while pregnant or breastfeeding then it is best to know your grower in effort to know your product, and please, use wisely!

Practice • Patience • Persistence

Alcohol – Similarly to herbs, everyone responds differently to alcohol based on their individual tolerance level. A safe rule to follow for alcohol consumption while breastfeeding is, *if you are sober enough to drive responsibly, then you are okay to breastfeed.*

Alcohol easily crosses into the breast milk, and it also easily transfuses out of the milk as well and returns to the mother's blood supply for elimination. Alcohol has a dehydrating effect on the body. Once a person rehydrates, the alcohol is released through the urine, saliva and sweat. For a breastfeeding mother, the alcohol can also be released through her breasts. Unfortunately, the more she expresses the more alcohol will flood the milk ducts. For this reason, *pumping and dumping* is not recommended. It is good to pump in small amounts for relief if you begin to feel engorged while sobering. However, the best method to eliminate alcohol is through the urine.

Cigarettes, Cigars, Hookah – Smoking of any kind is **not** recommended during breastfeeding. Nicotine does impact breast milk supply and in small amounts it will leech into the breast milk. The second-hand smoke either in the air or the smoke that remains on the clothes and skin is more harmful to baby than the amount found in the breast milk. It has been determined that a woman who smokes a pack of cigarettes daily is still safe to breastfeed her baby. Unfortunately, the nicotine tends to dehydrate thereby decreasing the milk supply. But breastfed babies are at lower risk for smoke related diseases compared to artificially fed babies, even when their mothers continue to smoke. Breastfeeding helps to protect babies from the potential risks of cigarette smoke.

Smoking & Breastfeeding
- La Leche League UK

> Breastfeeding is just as beneficial for the smoking mother and her baby as it is for the non-smoking mother and her baby. Research has shown that babies of smokers are at increased risk of colic, respiratory infections, and SIDS (Sudden Infant Death Syndrome or cot death).
>
> <u>But breastfed babies are at lower risk for these diseases compared to artificially fed ones, even when their mothers continue to smoke.</u> And breastfeeding helps to protect babies from the potential risks of cigarette smoke. Breastfeeding and smoking may well be less harmful to the child than bottle feeding and smoking.

If you are a smoker, be certain to always smoke outside away from your baby. Cover your hair and wear a designated robe or jacket while smoking. Be certain to remove these garments and wash your hands and face thoroughly after smoking and before engaging your baby. And always smoke after a feed, not before.

Birth Control – Breastfeeding suppresses estrogen production, slows ovulation, and stifles the libido, byway providing some protection from repeat pregnancies. However, breastfeeding is not a fully reliable form of birth control particularly if you begin to menstruate while nursing.

Synthetic birth control that is used to regulate ovulation tends to have unnatural side-effects in many women. Specifically, those containing progesterone can interfere with breast milk production. Spermicidal foams and gels can irritate a woman's vaginal ph. resulting in yeast infections, bacterial vaginosis and/or urinary tract infections. The intrauterine

Practice • Patience • Persistence

device, IUD, has greater risks to women of color as it can cause scar tissue to form around it, requiring surgical removal, and in some cases causing permanent damage.

Consider non-hormonal methods of birth control, such as condoms, diaphragms and/or the rhythm method. These methods require discipline! People have prevented pregnancies for thousands of years before the modern methods of birth control existed. Learn your body and your cycles. Abstain from sex or use condoms during your fertile days each month. Teach your partner about in-jaculation vs. ejaculation, whereas he can orgasm internally and preserve his semen.

Ejaculation vs. In-jaculation, Best Damn Prostate Book
-Ray Stone

> Many eastern cultures do not believe in losing any fluid from the body. Some practice a method of <u>retaining the semen and having orgasms without ejaculation</u>. Keeping the life force and nutrients inside of the body.
>
> Achieving this takes concentration and lots of practice; one must work on developing of the PC muscles in the body. If you are urinating and stop in the middle, the muscle that you'd use to stop the flow of urine is the PC (pubococcygeus) muscle. It can and should be exercised like any other muscle with a series of contractions.

NEVER Consume while Breastfeeding

The following should never be used while breastfeeding as they have been proven to cross into the milk supply in great amounts and can be harmful to your baby. There are cases of women breastfeeding while using street drugs and unfortunately the baby died because of these chemicals. In

Breastfeeding Essentials

some cases, these women were charged with manslaughter and faced prison time.

Many of the street drugs listed below are often laced into marijuana to make it more potent. If you are a smoker of marijuana, be responsible and always know the source of the herb. Never purchase pre-rolled marijuana and never socially smoke along-side strangers.

Street Drugs:

Barbiturates = Reds, Yellows, Barbs. Bluebirds, Blues, Toories, Downers, Pennies, Yellow Jackets, Blue Devils, Reds, Rainbows.

Cocaine = dust, happy dust, line, white lady, Mama Coca, chalk, candy, snow, kryptonite, blow etc. Cocaine is often laced in with marijuana.

Depressants = Backwards, blue heavens, downie, green dragons, joy juice, M&M, no worries, peanut, rainbows, red bullets, stoppers etc.

Heroin = brown sugar, smack, horse, Big H, junk, skunk, white horse or China white, black pearl, tar, etc. Heroin is also commonly laced in with marijuana and smoked.

Inhalants = laughing gas, air blast, moon gas, hard-on, honey oil, whippets, etc.

LSD (Lysergic acid diethylamide) = acid, black star, boomers, cubes, golden dragon, L, pink robots, superman, twenty-five, yellow sunshine, yin-yang, etc. LSD is often laced in with marijuana.

Practice • Patience • Persistence

MDMA (Methylenedioxy-methamphetamine) = Adam, bean, blue kisses, clarity, club drug, disco biscuits, E, ecstasy, hug drug, love drug, lover's speed, Mercedes, Molly, New Yorkers, peace, X, XTC, etc.

Methamphetamine = ice, blue devils, crank, fast, yellow powder, speed, Tina, glass, fire, chalk, etc.

Opium = big O, black stuff, Chinese tobacco, chocolate, hard stuff, hocus pocus, joy plant, O, zero, etc. Opium is sometimes laced in with marijuana.

OxyContin (oxycodone) = Kickers, Oxy, OC, Ox, Blues, Oxycotton

PCP (Phencyclidine) = angel dust, belladonna, black whack, CJ, cliffhanger, crystal joint, Detroit pink, elephant tranquilizer, hog, magic, Peter Pan, sheets, zoom. PCP is sometimes laced in with marijuana.

Psilocybin/psilocin = magic mushroom, Mexican mushrooms, mushrooms, musk, shrooms, silly putty, Simon, Simple Simon, etc.

Ritalin = crackers, poor man's heroin, R-ball, skippy, speedball, and Ritz, T's and R's, vitamin R, west coast, etc.

Rohypnol = circles, forget-me pill, la rocha, Mexican valium, R2, Reynolds, roofies, rope, wolfies, etc.

Syrup = Dex, Triple C, Velvet, Drank, Purple Drank, Sizzurp, Robo, Tussin, Orange Crush

Some Pharmaceutical Medicine. Many pharmaceutical medications are allowed while breastfeeding and pose no threat to the infant. However, there are a few listed below to be aware of. Unfortunately, commonly providers will suggest women discontinue breastfeeding while taking a certain prescription without the facts. I encourage you to become familiar with the LactMed® database, housed on the National Library of Medicine's Toxicology Data Network. It provides an *updated database of drugs and dietary supplements that may affect breastfeeding*.

Adderall = uppers, Addy's, Study Buddies, Dexies, Zing, Pep Pills, Black Beauties, Speed

Antineoplastic or Anticancer medication

Anticonvulsants or Antiepileptic medications = specific certain dosages of the following are not recommended while breastfeeding: Acetazolamide, Carbamazepine, Clonazepam, Ethosuximide, Lamotrigine, Nitrazepam, Phenobarbital, Primidone, Rufinamide, Tiagabine, Zonisamide, etc.

Ergot Alkaloids - dihydroergotamine, ergotamine, methysergide, dihydroergotamine, combinations, ergotamine, etc.

Radiopharmaceuticals and/or Chemotherapy medication. If you are a chemotherapy patient and undergoing treatments, then it is <u>not</u> recommended that you breastfeed.

Raw Honey given directly to infant under 12 months because it may contain spores of bacteria that can cause botulism which is a rare but serious gastrointestinal condition.

Practice • Patience • Persistence

Five Tips to Breastfeeding Success

Feed on Demand

There is much controversy over how often a baby should be breastfed, particularly a newborn. Many families are told to feed every 2-3 hours for about 15 minutes. This information is outdated and has led to poor weight gain in infants, which ultimately will require that infant to be supplemented. This idea, at times, makes me wonder if this model of breastfeeding was endorsed by formula companies. From birth you will witness your baby demonstrate behavior patterns known as feeding cues. These cues are a series of facial, hand, and other body gestures that alert the parents of a need to feed. Some of these body gestures are as follows:

- Waking up. Most newborns wake up from hunger.
- Lip and mouth smacking, sometimes while thrusting their tongue forward.
- Sucking or licking on hands.
- Turning their head to far right or far left, usually towards the mother's breast.
- If lying down the baby may attempt to squirm and move towards the mother.
- Crying is the final hunger cue.

A newborn baby within the first week of life must master their breathe-suck-swallow reflexes. Remember that this baby has never had to breathe before, nor eat. We easily take for granted our adult ability to do this simple mechanism – breathing and eating. For a newborn baby it is a great

Practice • Patience • Persistence

challenge, entirely stimulated by reflexes and requiring much of their focus. With every feed, your baby is learning and building muscle memory.

The first few days after birth a newborn feeding can easily be 30-45 minutes between both breasts. During these feedings, a baby's suckle is being motivated, not exclusively by hunger, but more by instinct. Once latched, this baby will take several pauses to breathe tenaciously, then continue to suckle and receive tiny drops of colostrum as a reward. In turn, this action helps to signal a mother's milk supply. Before the transitional milk presents (about 72 hours postpartum) it is ideal to encourage your baby to breastfeed every three hours. If your baby is not responsive to breastfeeding or rejects the breast after several attempts, then consult a lactation counselor, consultant, or pediatrician.

Once your transitional milk appears (about 72 hours postpartum) you will notice your baby having shorter feeds. However, your newborn is still processing breath-suck-swallow coordination and 20 - 30-minute feeding sessions are still normal. During this time, you will notice your baby's poop transition from a dark, sticky brownish color (meconium) to a runnier, greenish color.

This is a perfect time to begin feeding your baby on demand. Babies sometimes will display feeding habits similar to the parents. For the parent(s) who prefers to eat breakfast, lunch, dinner, and snacks in between, they may have a baby who will eat every 2-3 hours. For a parent(s) who simply likes to snack throughout the day, eating several small meals, your baby may be a grazer feeder. Whereas a feeding session can last almost an hour, your baby only suckles at 7 - 12-minute intervals and rests in between until full. There is also the once-a-day parent(s), who eats one meal a day. These babies will usually eat for longer periods of time and then have long nap periods in between.

As your baby grows, they will display a variety of feeding preferences that are greatly motivated by how they feel, both emotionally and physically. It was once believed that a baby's demand for milk increased during a growth spurt due to hunger, which consequently also increased a mother's milk supply. We now know that growth spurts are uncomfortable, causing aches and pains throughout the baby's body thereby urging them to seek the comfort of the breasts, and warmth and familiarity of the mother. Again, resulting in an increase of milk supply.

Similarly, when a baby feels insecure, frightened, sleepy, lonely, or in some cases boredom, then they will demand to feed. The ability to respond to these behavior changes in your baby can help to ensure you sustain a satiating milk supply during your breastfeeding journey.

No Artificial Nipples for the First Month.

In my practice, I have witnessed newborns from a few days postpartum to a few weeks young impressively transition from breast to bottle to breast again and not hurt the mother's nipples. However, they are rare, and those who present great challenges when given a bottle nipple within this same age range are more common. Many lactation professionals will advise parents to avoid giving their baby artificial nipples before one month of age. This is due to muscle memory and cognition. Our brains require

Practice • Patience • Persistence
---

approximately 21 days to wholistically retain, process, and execute new behavior patterns. Also, babies are born with a keen set of rooting and feeding reflexes which slowly become less responsive over time.

Artificial nipples alone are not the only culprit for disorienting a newborn's breastfeeding latch. There are other factors to consider, such as the baby's oral reflexes, the adult administering the bottle feed or pacifier, and gravity.

For decades, most bottles have been designed to stimulate the newborn's sucking reflex, located about a half inch to one inch deep at the roof of their mouths. This design was achieved knowing that once the sucking reflex is stimulated in the newborn that they will continue to respond by sucking continuously until the stimulation (bottle nipple) is removed.

A newborn also uses over 30 muscles and nerves to latch and stay attached to the breast during a feed. The average bottle only requires about 4-7 of these muscles to release the liquid contents.

Image 1. Common Bottle Feeding

Image 1 demonstrates the most common hold for bottle feeding a baby, whereas the bottle is being held vertically and the baby held in a reclined position. Though here the adult appears to be watching the baby feed, I have witnessed most bottle-feeding parents monitor the contents of the bottle and not the responses or cues of the baby. They will usually continue to feed the baby until the bottle is empty rather than watch the baby for signs of satiation.

In recent years, lactation professionals have discovered a technique of bottle feeding that greatly minimizes the potential of an infant being "nipple confused." Paced bottle feeding (Image 2) is quickly becoming the norm for bottle feeding a little one from birth to about six months when they begin to hold the bottle themselves. This technique allows for the baby to have more control over the feed and self-regulate their breathe-suck-swallow coordination without choking. Remember that digestion begins in the mouth and when babies are able to coordinate their breathing and swallowing then air is released appropriately from their bodies.

These feedings are usually longer and similar to breastfeeding. Baby is held in an upright position, as demonstrated in the image, which limits the force of gravity pooling milk into their mouths. The bottle is gently pushed deep into the baby's mouth to encourage their lips to flange around the nipple, similar to breastfeeding when their lips flange around the areola. Once the bottle is

Image 2. Paced Bottle Feeding

inserted appropriately inside of the baby's mouth, then baby in response will release their lower jaw muscle, causing the jaw to drop and trigger the tongue thrust reflex. The baby will then begin to mimic breastfeeding behavior on the bottle and the parent(s) are encouraged to give more attention to the baby's body language, which will indicate satiation.

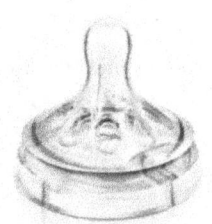

Image 3. Firm, rounded bottle nipple

To achieve paced bottle feeding you will need a slow-flow nipple with a firm, rounded end similar to image 3. Many of the bottles that offer wide-based nipples and/or curved-tip nipples will not function appropriately for this technique.

Pacifiers are another artificial nipple that breastfeeding families are encouraged to abstain from during the first month. Like bottle nipples, pacifier nipples are available in a variety of shapes and sizes. Unlike bottles, pacifiers were developed with the specific intent to keep your baby quiet and to stop your baby from crying. With this idea in mind, we must honor the fact that **babies cry for specific reasons**!

In January 2011, InCultureParent.com released an article titled, "Why African Babies Don't Cry." Within this article details are presented comparing the parenting traditions of many African cultures that require the mother to be very sensitive to the needs of her child. She is aware of the various sounds and gestures her baby gives to alert her of their needs before crying.

This research is important as it supports the fact that crying is a final form of communication a baby gives to alert their parents of a need. Crying is a desperate form of communication for hueman behavior. This is not intended to imply that your baby should never cry, that is unrealistic.

However, it is intended to give perspective of pacifier usage. As parents, it is your responsibility to learn this new person that has come into your lives. You must give attention to their body language and the various sounds they make. Granting this due diligence, you will hear that your baby has different sounds and gestures to relate hunger, discomfort, loneliness, fear, and even boredom.

As for pacifiers leading to "nipple confusion" in a breastfeeding infant, I have not witnessed this association in my practice. However, I have seen several cases of insufficient or slow weight gain in infants where parents routinely use pacifiers. Once the pacifiers were discontinued, and the mother was encouraged to "feed on demand," the infant quickly met weight gain expectations. In some cases, the mother experienced an increase in milk supply as well.

Stay Hydrated & Rest

Hueman milk is high in lactose which requires great amounts of water for production. Though recent research tells us that hueman milk is not dependent on what a mother eats, it is however dependent on what she drinks. In essence, every beverage we consume is converted to water within our bodies. Our kidneys do an incredible job at filtering water from sodas, coffee, juice, tea, Kool-Aid, milk, etc.

During breastfeeding, if you are not consuming adequate amounts of fluid then your body will first rob your skin and hair of moisture. Some women experience extra dry skin, brittle nails, and flakiness of the scalp. Others may have consistent dry mouth and dry vaginal irritation. If the dehydration

Practice • Patience • Persistence

continues, she will eventually experience low milk supply. It is necessary to consume the daily requirements of liquids which is half your body weight in ounces. For example, if you weigh 160 pounds then your daily fluid consumption should be 80 oz. (10 cups). Fortunately, many breastfeeding women tend to feel thirstier and will drink more fluids naturally. Be intentional to make water a minimum of half your daily beverage consumption.

Hueman lactation is more stable and predictable than many believe it to be. Nature ensures the lifecycle for mammals by providing milk substance for the duration of nursing. Whether this duration is a few weeks or a few years, the fountain of youth continues to produce so long as there is a demand.

We must realize that self-preservation is also a Law of Nature, which is instinctive self-defense when threatened. The point I'm making is that stressors can have an impact on breast milk production. The hueman body is consistently working to maintain a balanced state of health referred to as homeostasis. This relates to every system and cell of our bodies, as well as mental and emotional health. If the body is struggling to balance homeostasis, then it is likely to conserve and redirect energy required for breast milk production towards restoring the host's systems.

If breast is best, then so is rest.

As a mother I realize how difficult it can seem to rest when you feel you have so many demands to meet. Being a black woman in America makes resting an even greater challenge, especially when you are a transplant to

Breastfeeding Essentials

a non-native city or state, where you are without close family. Also, if you are a working mother, business owner, and/or if you have other little ones to care for, then the idea of resting after birth can seem delusional or unrealistic. Resting can feel even more impossible if you are a single mom or co-parent. However, the reality is that resting during the first year postpartum is critical, and you must make intentional rest times a ritualistic part of your day.

Be reminded that it can take as long as 42 weeks to bring forward another hueman being. There are only 52 weeks in a year. This process takes from the mother's calcium deposits (bones, teeth, hair, nerves), iron storage (blood supply), proteins (muscle, brain), and water reserves (whole body). Pregnancy in all its beauty and majesty is a full body stressor on the mother. This is evident by many of the unfortunately common pregnancy related issues that women experience. For these reasons, and others not mentioned here, it is necessary to honor time after birth to allow your whole being to rest and heal.

Breast milk production is a co-dependency process. Mom needs baby to manage the supply and baby needs mom for sustenance. During a feeding, endorphins or "feel-good" hormones are released to help the mother relax and the milk to flow. When she honors this process by sitting and holding her baby, her body responds with sufficient milk let down. When she is distracted, agitated, or stressed, then the opposite is likely to occur.

As a traditional midwife and lactation consultant, I have counseled many millennial moms on the importance of slowing down and making time to complete a feed with her baby. Our society is rapidly advancing with

Practice • Patience • Persistence

computers and technology. Many of us are fortunate to live in industrialized countries and have access to a great number of conveniences that make life more comfortable. Washing machines, driers, dish washers, heaters, water heaters, refrigerators, computers, television, etc... With all this advancement one would expect us to have more time to share with our babies and loved ones. However, our reality is the peculiar opposite. Women living in developing countries actually have more time with their babies and families. They work together daily to manage a living of gathering food, water, and wood along with cooking, cleaning, and walking. Their babies are typically attached to them during their daily activities and many rest times are reserved to tend to the needs of their babies and themselves. The strange irony to our lives as Americans is, we are loyal to a system and work extensively to maintain luxuries that inevitably rob our lives of irreplaceable and invaluable time. Contrary to a popular saying, we cannot "make time" and we do not "have time." We are essentially integrated with time, and it is our choice as to what we do within it. So as a breastfeeding mother nurture yourself and your baby within your time.

The time required to breastfeed your baby is very short by comparison to the potential extent of their lives. Consider that your baby will grow more extensively within the first year after birth than they will for the remainder of their lifetime. Which makes this first year an even more critical time to literally invest in the future of your baby's health.

Care for your Breasts

Many of the breastfeeding discomforts that women experience can be prevented or minimized by simply caring for your breasts regularly. If you are like me, breastfeeding was the most activity my breasts have ever experienced on a consistent and daily basis. The breasts are being handled eight or more times a day in a seemingly non-gentle and demanding manner, by a little person who quickly assumes ownership of them. In most cases this little person is not obliged to share the breasts and can be quite hostile about access to the breasts at their own leisure.

My first breastfeeding experience was the most challenging for me. It was a great adjustment because I had so little knowledge and even fewer examples. I only had my confidence and inner knowing that women breastfed for thousands of years before me and that I too could do it. The challenges I endured of thrush, mastitis, clogged milk ducts, sore and damaged nipples (all discussed in chapter 6), demanded that I give extra attention to how I cared for my breasts. As I tended to each issue and healed, I was also learning how to prevent these uncomfortable setbacks.

Caring for your breasts is as simple as being intentional between feeds to feel and look at your breasts. Give the twins (breasts) a daily massage. Massaging them not only gives you an opportunity to check for lumps but when coupled with deep breathing it is incredibly healing. Use a nipple cream or butter generously on your nipples to help seal in moisture and prevent cracks. Go braless a much as possible to allow adequate blood circulation and opportunities for your breast tissues to breath. Avoid bras with underwire as they can lead to mastitis, which is an infection of a milk duct or gland (page 89). These bras and tight bras can restrict milk ducts and glands from proper expulsion of the milk, causing clogs.

As you wash your breast, take care to avoid applying soap directly to your nipples and areola. The soaps can strip away vital oils being released by the Montgomery Glands which are divinely designed to help protect the nipples from cracking and chafing. Nature has already equipped our bodies, as other mammals, with a natural oil substance that protects our nipples from the baby's saliva. This natural oil also doubles as an antiseptic to prevent infection. Unfortunately, many of the soaps we use remove this natural oil.

> *Additional thoughts to consider about breast health.
> There has been some growing controversy over the idea of bras, specifically those containing underwire, potentially leading to breast cancer. The assumption is that the underwire or bras that fit too tight, restrict the lymph nodes located under the breasts from properly releasing protective blood cells that would otherwise keep the breasts healthy. Though this idea is very persuasive, it is not endorsed by science. Apparently, there isn't "substantial evidence," or funding, to substantiate these claims.
>
> Likewise, antiperspirants are also under attack for similar reasoning. The idea here is that the chemicals in underarm antiperspirants that are absorbed through the skin, interfere with lymph circulation, and cause toxins to build up in the breast, eventually leading to breast cancer (American Cancer Society). Again, this idea isn't supported by science due to lack of evidence.

Breastfeeding Essentials

What we do know:
1. The breasts are a part of the reproductive system and house mammary glands which are responsible for milk production.
2. Huemans are the only mammals that wear bras.
3. Tight Bras are uncomfortable and do restrict blood circulation.
4. Certain synthetic fabrics such as, rayon, polyester, acrylic, acetate, and nylon, can leech unhealthy chemicals into the skin. Coincidentally these are the fibers most bras are made from.
5. While breastfeeding or lactating, tight bras and underwire can lead to mastitis, which is a breast infection, as they impede proper expulsion of the milk.
6. Sweat is a vital part of the body's excretory system whereas toxins are released from the body.
7. There are lymph nodes located directly under the breasts and armpits as a vital part of our body's defense system.

In the words of renowned Grand Midwife, UmmSalaamah Sondra Abdullah-Zaimah, "*Science has yet to catch up with common sense*".... So you decide!

Breast cancer rates are increasing and affecting black American women at an alarming rate. We are 40% times more likely to die from breast cancer than other ethnic groups. Much of this is due to late detection. I will not drudge on with more alarming statistics about breast cancer, as I am certain we all know someone affected by this dis-ease. I will however employ you to be intentional about Breast Care. **LOVE ON YOUR BREASTS!** Not in an intimate sense (though that is fun too) but with healing intentions. Breast care must continue beyond breastfeeding. Our breasts have astounding ability to collect toxins and hold stress, just as our wombs. Massaging them not only gives you an opportunity to check for lumps and other invaders, but when coupled with deep breathing it is

Practice • Patience • Persistence

incredibly healing. Here are some motivational facts about breast massage:

- Helps fight breast cancer!!
- Encourages the release of feel-good hormones like oxytocin and relaxin.
- Stimulates anti-aging hormones such as prolactin and estrogen!
- Encourages more red blood circulation.
- Helps to fight foreign invaders and infectious disease.
- Encourages fuller more perky breasts!

So, go ahead ladies and feel'em up every day! You deserve it!

Securing a "Good" Latch

I find this section of the book to be more challenging to explain, so in this section I will steer from directives and expertise. Latching a newborn baby to your breast is where we in the lactation support community see a line drawn in the sand between those who will persist and those who will quit. Those who will become adept pumpers and those who will switch to formula.

Most literature on latching a newborn presents step by step techniques. They typically imply that if you follow their method correctly then the latch should be comfortable and effective. Unfortunately, I have witnessed several situations whereas mom is following the rules of engagement to the best of her ability and the latch just is not working for her. I truly feel latching is intuitive for both mom and baby. Each are on a mission to meet a need; mom to express milk and baby to drink milk; mom is seeking relief and baby is seeking fulfillment. If the latch is uncomfortable to mom, then it is most likely uncomfortable to baby. This is evident in the mouths and lips of babies with poor latches. They will often display a callus or bruise on the lips, tongue, or gums from poor latching.

I have witnessed women latch their babies in what would appear to a trained eye to be incredibly uncomfortable. Where baby's head is completely turned to the left or right and only latched to her nipple. Mom is supporting her breast with the *cigarette hold*, or not supporting her breast at all. I can also hear audible slurps and smacking from baby which clearly indicates baby is swallowing air, yet baby does not display any of the expected side effects such as gas or spitting up. When I ask the mother "how does the latch feel", she responds that it feels fine and comfortable.

On the contrary, I have seen what can be described as a *perfect latch* to a trained eye. Baby is facing the breast with mouth fully engaged on the areola and lips flanged wide like a guppy fish. No audible sounds other than rhythmic swallows. Yet this mom is experiencing brow raising, toe-curling pain. She latches baby with perfect aim to the nose, encouraging baby to open wide and lift their neck to allow mom's nipple to land deep into their mouths. Mom also breaks the latch perfectly by inserting her finger along the side of baby's mouth to release the suction and not damage her nipple. When I ask this mom the same question, "how does the latch feel," she replies that it is painful.

To teach a woman how to properly latch can be challenging. Ideally this should be an intuitive process for both mom and baby. When we look at mammals in nature, no one has to teach the mother how to latch her offspring. The female figures it out somehow, and if the latch is painful, she will push the offspring away. Ultimately the offspring must learn to latch comfortably if it desires to survive. Similarly, with huemans, "baby-led latching" is being encouraged more throughout the lactation support community. Observers have witnessed that when newborns are allowed time to find the nipple, then they do so effectively.

The take-away note here is to allow your newborn baby *time* to first acclimate to this highly sensitizing environment, then allow them time to find your breasts. Adults living in industrial cities tend to lack this very essential life component. Most of our lifestyles are conducted within time sensitive schedules. From school, to work, to home, we are constantly rushing. Newborns are primitive. They function on a very primitive and self-centered timeline. A time before internet, computers, phones, cars, and electricity (that we know of). A time when we were striking stones together for fire and gathering food from the wild.

Even in our best effort to allot babies time for bonding and breastfeeding, we only give them the "Golden Hour" of birth. This is laughable! Unmedicated newborns can stay awake for up to six hours immediate postpartum. The average is three, but this is still much longer than an hour. Baby Friendly Hospitals throughout the U.S. are encouraged to grant parents this "Golden Hour" with their newborn baby as if it were a courtesy. Unfortunately, this first hour postpartum is usually chaotic. The delivery room is filled with people, mainly strangers. Mom's perineum or bottom is being inspected and possibly repaired, then cleaned. The bedding may be changed or restored. All while either dad, partner, doula, a family member, or someone other than mom is holding the baby. Once the chaos has settled and several of the strangers have left the room, mom is then given her baby briefly before being harassed by a Neo-Natal Nurse claiming, "It has been an hour now since birth and I need to examine and wash the baby."

All this interference can be crippling to a mother's breastfeeding journey. It delays both mom's and baby's instincts to bond and breastfeed. By the time mom receives her baby, swaddled like a burrito, they both are usually too tired to pursue nursing. The next opportunity to feed will be hours later when baby wakes from hunger pains or symptoms thereof. These newly felt sensations can be very overwhelming to their immature primitive brains. Remember that your baby has never experienced hunger, or breathing, or being cold or hot, bright lights, or even touch on certain body parts. All of these sensations can be overwhelming to their senses and cause them to cry inconsolably.

Now baby is screaming and uncooperative with breastfeeding. For a new mom who desires greatly to give her baby the best, she is now feeling defeated. She attempts to nurse using whatever method she has learned and if baby does not "latch" appropriately after several attempts, then she is most likely to surrender to the *Ready-Made* formula already positioned under the hospital bassinet in her postpartum room. If the formula is not available in the room, then it is only a nurse call button away.

This first feed can make a serious difference in your success as a breastfeeding mother. Hueman babies, like all mammals, are born with instincts and reflexes to seek out the teat. It is greatly believed that this

Practice • Patience • Persistence

instinct is not hunger driven, but primally motivated by survival. They follow the smell and taste of amniotic fluid emanating from the mother's linear negra (dark line on mother's abdomen extending from her naval to her pubis) and chest area. From here their reflexes to crawl and root take over which eventually guide them to the breasts.

A non-medicated mother's instincts will also surface when left uninterrupted. She will intuitively guide her baby to her breasts and assist him/her with latching. This may look different for each woman depending on a variety of factors. Culture, confidence, exposure to other breastfeeding women, and even the size of her breasts can dictate how a mother will guide her baby during those first feeds.

A few suggestions for the first feeds:

- Ask your attending nurse and/or provider to delay the initial newborn tests and exams until after the first feed.
- Hold your baby skin-to-skin between your breasts.
- Allow your baby to suck on their hands and lick at your chest while searching for the breast.
- When you feel ready then assist your baby with finding the desired breast.
- When baby latches it should not hurt. It may however feel like a mild pinch and/or pulling sensation at the nipple.

If the latch is uncomfortable then insert one of your fingers into the side crease of the baby's mouth until the latch seal is broken. Remove your nipple and try again.

Solutions for 9 Common Breastfeeding Concerns

Practice • Patience • Persistence

Many of the breastfeeding discomforts that women experience can be prevented or minimized by simply caring for your breasts regularly. Routine breast care ideas are detailed in chapter 6 under *Care for your Breasts*. This section will cover nine most common concerns or issues that can arise during your breastfeeding journey.

Engorgement

Engorgement may very well be the most common breastfeeding concern among both new moms and veteran moms. Engorgement has a simple meaning: to be bulged, gorged, inflamed, or filled to capacity. However, as it relates to breastfeeding, it refers to the breasts being painfully overfull, firm and/or swollen. The common implication here is that the breasts are overfilled with milk, yet this is not always the case. With the increased use of intravenous fluid (IV fluid) during labor, birth and immediate postpartum, this is now a very relative variable to consider when dealing with engorgement.

During pregnancy, a woman has an estimated 50% bodily fluid increase, with exception to the amniotic fluid which is immediately released during birth. The remaining excess fluid will be released through the excretory system via sweat, urine and breast milk. Some lactation professionals believe this extra body fluid increase is created to directly help with breast milk production within the first few weeks postpartum since mature breast milk is predominantly water.

As the body works to maintain homeostasis (balance) after birth it must minimize this excess body fluids presence around major organs (brain, heart, liver, and others). This is when the extremities become storage areas and many women will see swelling, or continued swelling, of the feet, hands, and now, breasts. Much of the engorgement women see during the first week postpartum is a result of several liters of IV fluid that was poured into their bodies during delivery. This fluid is called interstitial or extracellular fluid (fluid that accumulates around the outside of the cell's body). This extracellular fluid compounds the issue of engorgement. The breast tissue has already grown one to two cup sizes during pregnancy to make space for the expected mature milk, but they are not prepared for the sudden presence of extra fluid from the IV fluid. These moms usually experience breasts swelling as early as 24 hours postpartum, and this swelling is easily mistaken for mature milk. The body quickly occupies the accessible breasts space with excess fluid as it works to balance post-birth dynamics. You can imagine that within 72 hours postpartum, when the transitional milk begins to take form, the breasts are overfull or engorged. Usually to the capacity where the breast skin is stretched and shiny like a full balloon, and her nipples appear stretched and flat like the opposing side of a balloon where it is inflated.

The best relief for this type of swelling is anti-inflammatory foods (ginger, pineapples, celery, kale, beets berries), herbs/spices (rosemary, turmeric, cinnamon, clove, chamomile) and medicine (ibuprofen up to 800mg).

Alternating warm and cold compresses can also be helpful with engorgement. Use a warm compress before a feeding or pumping to help expand the vessels and release the milk. Use a cold compress after a feed

Practice • Patience • Persistence

---

to constrict the vessels and encourage your body to metabolize the extracellular fluid into the excretory system for sweat or urine.

Breastfeed as much as baby will entertain you. It can be helpful to hand express prior to latching to allow more surface area around the nipple for baby to latch. Your partner can also prove helpful in achieving this by sucking some of the milk out. Their suckle tends to be more effective as well.

Rest and relax! This too shall pass! Have a clean towel nearby for naps as you will most likely leak. The best thing you can do when met with parenting challenges as your child grows is: 1. remember that this experience is only temporary 2. allow the experiences to be learning opportunities. Learn how your body functions and what works best for your whole being and your baby.

Clogged Milk Duct

At some time during your breastfeeding journey, you will most likely experience a clogged milk duct. The name is the definition. The most common cause of clogged milk duct(s) is inefficient milk removal, or a premature nursing routine. A premature nursing routine is switching breasts before it has completed a full milk ejection cycle or let-down.

Most diagrams of mammary gland anatomy depict the ductal system as a simple straight pathway leading towards the outlet (nipple). However, the ductal pathway is more coiled than straight, and it twists and spirals towards the outlet. This depiction is important because it helps us to overstand how the ducts become clogged.

The fat of breast milk, though minimal, is composed of long chain fatty acids (polyunsaturated) and short chain fatty acids (SCFAs). As milk moves through the coiled ductal system towards the outlet, the short SCFAs move more rapidly along with the water as it has less mass. The longer chains, on the contrary, have greater mass and can easily become lodged in the coils creating a clog as milk builds behind it. When the breast is stimulated efficiently, either with baby or pump, then these clogs are relieved with adequate force (suction, massage, pressure). When the stimulation is stopped abruptly, with premature nursing routines, the clog remains, which can develop into mastitis.

Clogged milk ducts are avoidable with routine breast care. Your breasts are working and performing magnificently to provide sustenance for your baby(s). Reward them with love and care. Make time daily to gently massage your breasts and loosen the internal tissues. Address any unusual lumps with warm compresses and deep tissue massage. This will help to relieve the clogs. If you do this prior to feeding or pumping it is even more effective.

Another preventative measure is to allow your breasts to complete a full ejection reflex cycle before switching breasts. As you learn your body's lactation process, you will witness how your breasts release milk. They begin with a trickle that can persist from a few seconds to a few minutes. This trickle then becomes more rapid as if a faucet has been opened slightly more. For many women this can appear as a spray, like a shower.

After several minutes of this rapid pouring of milk, you will witness the flow return to a trickle then a drip.

This milk ejection cycle is different for every woman and can range from 5 to 20 minutes. I have witnessed women breastfeed for seven minutes and the baby's post-feed weight reveals three ounces transferred. On the contrary I have witnessed women breastfeed 15 minutes and only one ounce transferred. In which case (depending on age of the baby) I encourage her to return baby to the same breast for next feeding. Your breast should feel significantly softer before switching. It is also a good habit to massage your breast during a feed; specifically, if you feel a lump present.

A more uncommon cause of clogged milk duct(s) is trauma, usually caused by over-pumping. This scenario is a clog caused by inflammation. Moms have helped me realize this type of clog. They describe the lump or clog as feeling tender or sore during massage and irritated during a feeding or pumping. Sometimes the area appears reddish and warm. This type of clogged milk duct can easily be mistaken and treated as mastitis, which will be explained later. The primary difference is no infection is present, hence the absence of any flu-like symptoms.

Remember the ductal system is directly connected to the outlet (nipple). Over-stimulation not only irritates the nipples but also impacts the integrity of the ductal system. During the milk ejection reflex, oxytocin stimulates specific muscles to contract and squeeze the ducts, thereby expressing the milk within. The theory here is too much friction caused by artificial stimulation or pumping irritates the duct causing it to inflame.

Breastfeeding and massaging only aggravates this inflamed duct more. The best relief is a warm compress before a feed, and a cold compress after a feed. Minimize activity of the affected breast until the swelling has resolved. Meaning no massaging or pumping. Also ingest anti-inflammatories such as: foods (ginger, pineapples, celery, kale, beets berries), herbs/spices (rosemary, turmeric, cinnamon, clove, chamomile) and medicine (ibuprofen up to 800mg).

Sore nipples/bruised nipples

Most breastfeeding moms will experience some nipple soreness as her breasts adapt to having consistent attention. For this reason, again, routine breast care can be of great benefit for prevention. Make a habit of expressing a few drops of milk after a feed and rub the milk onto your nipple. Allow the nipples to airdry before covering them. You can also apply any edible oil (such as olive oil, grapeseed oil, coconut oil, etc.) to help seal in moisture.

Once nipples become bruised and traumatized, breastfeeding is no longer fun. It quickly becomes this dreaded task, and your cute little baby becomes this horrid suction monster. I have seen moms persevere through the pain and latch their little ones onto a red, scabbing, blistered nipple. This is counterproductive to healing and only further traumatizes the damaged nipple.

If your nipples are sore to the point of pain while nursing, you definitely want to seek out the counsel of a breastfeeding specialist to help determine the cause. In the meantime, you can use the following recommendations from *La Leche League*

- Freshly expressed breast milk applied to your nipples will soothe them and reduce the chances of infection, as hueman milk has antibacterial properties. (Do not use if thrush is present.)
- Apply warm, moist compresses to your nipples (if a yeast infection is not present).
- Keep your nipples covered with a (100% pure) lanolin ointment or hydrogel dressing to encourage any cracks to heal without scabbing or crusting.
- Offer your baby short, frequent feedings to encourage a less vigorous suck. Nurse on the least sore side first, if possible.
- When removing your baby from your breast, break the suction gently by pulling on baby's chin or insert clean finger at corner of mouth.

In your internet hunt for relief suggestions from Dr. Google, be cautious of some ideas such as applying moist tea bags to the nipples which has been proven to have an astringent effect that may promote drying and cracking. Also, at one time it was recommended that a hair dryer or sunlamp be used on sore nipples. Research has now shown that this also promotes drying and further cracking; however, direct sunlight can be incredibly healing for bruised or traumatized nipples. Natural sunlight stimulates the body to synthesize vitamin D which instantly causes specific immune cells to travel to the outer layers of the skin for both protection and healing.

Non-latching Baby

The most important fact to remember about a non-latching baby is they want to eat, and they prefer their mother's milk over any other food. If your baby is rejecting your breasts, then there is a reason beyond the aforementioned causes. The best option here is to seek counsel with a lactation professional to determine why your baby has problems latching. This section highlights some of the more common reasons why a baby will refuse to latch.

A newborn is genetically programmed and equipped with many reflexes to find the teat, latch, and suckle. When this process is disrupted, as described in chapter 6 under Latching, then the margin of error begins to grow wider, and confidence tends to greatly decrease.

If a newborn is rejecting the breast nipple and no artificial nipple, such as a bottle or pacifier, has been introduced then we can first consider the breastfeeding position. Be certain that baby is being held at close range to the breast and the nipple is aimed towards baby's nose. Be mindful not to push your baby's head against your breast. Instead allow your baby's head to have flexibility to use their range of motion muscles within the neck and to open their jaw. If baby is attempting to latch to the breast but has challenges attaching, then you can consider the nipple shape.

Nipple shape can influence the quality of the latch. If a nipple has minimal surface area, better known as *short nipples*, then baby may experience challenges with attaching or maintaining a latch. In this scenario I encourage mothers to pinch the areola around the nipple to make it more elongated. This can help to give baby more surface area to latch.

Practice • Patience • Persistence

If we have a newborn baby at the breast and they appear to struggle with coordination, whereas the breast is at the right of their face, but they are turning to the left, or baby opens their mouth but won't thrust their tongue to latch, then we can consider baby having improper neural responses. It can also be sore muscles or bruised tissues from birth. Chiropractors remind us that pregnancy and birth can impact the nervous system of the baby by way of the spinal cord. In which case you can consider infant massage, oral exercises and/or visiting a chiropractor that adjusts babies.

Some babies prefer to be swaddled for the first week or so after birth. These babies usually have over-active startle reflexes and will cry inconsolably when their arms are free. They appear to reject the breast because they will fight and cry while mom is trying to feed. A nice and tight swaddle can help these little ones feel secure and more focused on latching.

When a baby is persistently refusing to latch and cries upon assuming the breastfeeding position, or seeing the breast, then the most common reason is they have developed a negative connotation with breastfeeding. I encourage and commend a family's determination to breastfeed. I also caution these same families to be creative and patient with their little one. If the feed is presenting with challenges, take breaks and hold your baby skin-to-skin. Sing, talk, rock, and dance with your baby to help them and you stay calm. Once baby has calmed down then attempt to feed again. If for whatever unknown reason your baby is not latching, then pump and practice paced bottle feeding instead (chapter 6). Try again next feed. Most importantly, keep a positive attitude about your breastfeeding journey and seek out the help of a lactation professional. Remember your baby shares a bio-chemical and bio-rhythmic relation with you as the mother. When you are stressed and release stress-related hormones, your baby can smell those hormones and sense that something is wrong. Their immature brains cannot interpret what is wrong. Their minds interpret danger and no longer feel safe in your arms. I know this can be stressful but know that this too shall pass.

Gassy/Colicky Baby

Gas or flatulence in newborns is a common byproduct of digestions. If your baby is burping and passing the gas naturally then there is no cause for alarm. Colic, however, is when the gas, for whatever reason, is obstructed in the intestines and causing abdominal pain. Colic in your baby usually presents with intense crying and a distended or hard-feeling abdomen. Your baby may try to curl into a fetal position with their hands clutched in a fist, due to the abdominal discomfort. Digestion and elimination are new phenomena for newborns. Some babies will startle themselves with their own gas and bowel sounds. As the milk travels through the pathway of the baby's digestive system, the sensation can be unfamiliar to some causing them to cry. Most newborn babies will experience an episode of colic due to having an immature digestive system. At birth, your baby has only had amniotic fluid in their system. After birth, colostrum helps to coat their digestive system with a serum of probiotics and antibiotics along with other healing agents helping to prepare their bodies for mature milk. This is a leading factor as to why colic is more prevalent in formula-fed babies. Their digestive system was robbed of this critical opportunity to be primed by colostrum.

Contrary to popular opinion, breast milk does not easily cause gas and colic in babies. The breast milk production pathway is incredibly intricate and divinely designed, so that few of the essential properties within the foods you consume will ever reach your baby's digestive system. Still, it is better for a mom to continue to eat as she did during pregnancy while breastfeeding. In utero your baby was exposed to many of the subtle flavors and enzymes from the foods you ate so it's better to keep your eating pattern consistent.

Colic is usually caused by over-eating or swallowing too much air. Breastfed babies can and do over-eat, especially if the mom is an over-producer. This can cause the baby to eat more than needed out of convenience or availability. Much like adults at an all you can eat buffet.

Colic can also be triggered by mothers with forceful let-downs that cause her baby to gulp and choke. These babies tend to take in too much air along with the milk, disorienting their breathe-suck-swallow coordination. Instead, these babies gulp-gulp-gulp-gasp for air. It can be helpful for these mothers to hand-express 1-2 minutes of the initial let-down prior to latching baby. Most babies will eventually adapt to their mother's milk flow.

Bottle-feeding can certainly cause colic. It is very easy to overfeed a baby with a bottle and the average bottle nipple will disorient a newborn's breathe-suck-swallow coordination (refer to chapter 6, No Artificial Nipples for first month).

Breastfeeding Essentials

What most parents believe to be colic in their newborn in most cases is just a fussy baby. The most common causes for fussy babies are anxious mommas. Moms who ae stressed, sad, irritable, or busy. Remember that for the first year or more a baby is dependent upon the biorhythms and biochemistry of the mother. They rely on mom to help sleep, regulate vitals, and even interpret danger. When a woman is stressed, her body naturally releases cortisol, or stress hormones. The baby can smell these hormones. These cortisol hormones also increase the mother's vitals, so her heart rate and breathing are now more rapid. In turn this increases the baby's vitals. As the mother's fight or flight system is stimulated, baby is now in a state of insecurity and need. The only comfort for your baby in this state is being held, preferably by someone who is calm.

I recall being jealous and resentful that my mother could instantly calm my babies after I had been trying for a significant length of time. There were moments when I thought my baby did not like me. Not knowing that it was my own insecurities, impatient rocking and frustrated energy that was causing him or her to cry.

Another colic misconception is irritable baby syndrome a.k.a witching-hours. This is described as a specific and consistent time of the day or night when your baby is inconsolably crying. Science does not support this syndrome and refers to it as theoretical. However, I experienced this with two of my babies and it was very real for me and their father. For both girls, their onset of tantrum would be at night between 8pm and midnight. They each started presenting this behavior about 2 – 3 weeks postpartum and continued until about two months. For me, the consistency of timing was the most peculiar. I can only assure you that this syndrome is real and encourage you to be creative and patient with this growing pain. A few suggestions to help with this syndrome are:

- Infant massage to help sooth any aching muscles.
- Warm baby baths infused with a few drops of lavender essential oil.
- Late evening walks outside while holding your baby.
- Dancing while holding your baby.
- You can drink calming herbal teas (chamomile, catnip, linden, valerian) an hour or two prior to the timing of their onset, then breastfeed. Watch for bowel tolerance.
- Be certain to have a partner nearby to trade-off when you begin to feel overwhelmed.
- Know that this too shall pass!

Low Milk Supply

The most common cause of low milk supply is disrupted feedings or inadequate stimulation. The leading cause for mothers to discontinue breastfeeding worldwide is due to a lack of confidence in her milk supply. Mothers somehow disconnect their body's incredible potential to co-create and support an entire hueman being for nearly a year in-utero, from her continued ability to produce milk in effort to sustain this little hueman. In short, moms, if you can grow a baby then you can surely produce the milk (This is in assumption that there are no underlying medical conditions.) I

Breastfeeding Essentials

like to first affirm this notion in women and allow them to feel confident in their body's greatness.

When confronted with a concern of low milk supply, we must take the time to assess the entire breastfeeding experience, from birth to current. Several factors must be considered, such as: the age of the baby; was this birth a C-section; is the baby supplementing with formula; and is the mother taking any birth control or other medications that can inhibit milk production. We also must know if there is an underlying medical condition such as diabetes, PCOS or hypoplasia (underdevelopment of breast tissue), or a her-story of breast surgeries such as implants or reductions.

With the before mentioned considered and ruled out, an occasional bout with low milk supply is relatively common. Newborn growth spurts, illness and menstruation can each reduce breast milk supply. Newborn growth spurts occur about 7-10 days postpartum, then again about 2-3 weeks and 4-6 weeks. Babies also spurt around 3 months, 4 months, 6 months, and 9 months. During a growth spurt, many moms feel like they are not producing enough because babies can be more demanding due to a need for comfort. In this scenario, it is best to increase your fluids, eat more healthy snacks and have intentional rest times. In most cases after 2-3 days baby should return to their normal feeding routine.

The same regimen should be incorporated for illness such as colds and the flu. As the body attempts to fight off invading viruses, the best thing a mother can do is rest and stay hydrated. CONTINUE BREASTFEEDING AS USUAL since your baby has already been exposed to your cold or flu germs. As your body works to create antibodies, then these same antibodies will be shared freely through your breast milk.

Menstruation also has the direct ability to reduce milk supply because it is a time when a woman's body is losing blood. Breast milk is dependent upon a woman's blood supply for production. It is, in essence, a blood byproduct. If you are menstruating and breastfeeding, then you want to be very intentional about resting. If you are working, plan an off day during the first and/or second day of your moon time. This time is sacred and should be honored as such! Specific self-care routines such as warm baths, yoni steaming, and womb massage are necessary during your moon time. Your body is naturally cleansing itself so select nutrient-rich foods to replace what is loss. This is a time to eat lots of green salads, hearty soups, and various fruits. Drink herbal teas designed by nature to help aid the female's reproductive system and enrich blood supply, such as red raspberry leaf, nettles, alfalfa, fenugreek, milk thistle and oatstraw). You will notice that by honoring your moon time (menstruation) and caring for your body appropriately that your milk supply will sustain better as well.

Underweight Baby

Similar to low breast milk supply, there are several reasons a baby can be below their expected weight gain. It seems socially convenient to blame the mother's breast milk when there is an issue with baby. Specifically, as it relates to digestive upset, skin issues, inconsolable crying, jaundice, and low or slow weight gain. Breast milk can be an easy target when issues arise in baby. Yet there are many underlying causes for the before mentioned issues.

When a new baby is not meeting their expected weight gain milestones, I first look at the birth weight vs. the baby's weight at discharge from the hospital (or the 48-hour weight). Remember that a newborn baby has been suspended in fluid since conception which inflates the birth weight. Newborn babies will release this extra fluid via urine over the first 48 hours, making the discharge weight check more accurate. It is important to recognize the difference in weight checks in the event you are challenged by your pediatrician about insufficient weight gain.

Weight loss in newborns is to be expected, as they can lose as much as 10% of their birth weight. Meaning if your baby's birth weight was 7 pounds 5 ounces (3.4kg) then a weight loss of up to 0.75lb (0.34kg) is acceptable over the first week postpartum. Making this baby's weight about 6.75lb (3.06kg). However, your baby is expected to regain this weight within two weeks of birth. Many parents are pressured at the one-week postpartum pediatric visit to encourage newborn weight gain either by pumping or using formula. This can be shattering to the confidence of a newly breastfeeding mom.

Before rushing to formula or encouraging a mother to pump at one-week postpartum, I first look at the baby's 48-hour weight. A baby born at 7.5lb (3.4kg) can easily weigh 7lb (3.1kg) within 48-hours. Meaning at one week if baby's weight is 6.3lb (2.79kg) then we are still within expected range of weight loss. The average person would look at the birth weight and panic seeing this baby has loss over a pound within first week, neglecting the fact

Practice • Patience • Persistence

that as much as five ounces of that total birth weight was fluff from amniotic fluid; and if the mother received several litters of IV fluid during labor, then this can inflate baby's weight as well.

We also must consider the fact that before the first week postpartum a newborn's belly is very small and can scarcely hold one fluid ounce (30ml) per feed. After which time a baby is expected to gain an estimated one ounce (28.3g) per day.

Beyond birth weight discrepancies, slow weight gain in newborns can be a concerning issue for parents. I have witnessed many families using infant formula and/or discontinue breastfeeding due to insufficient weight gain in baby. Rarely is a mother's diet the cause, but the mother's supply can be. It is difficult to measure the amount of milk a woman is producing by pumping alone. This is because babies can remove more milk from the breast than a breast pump. The best measure of a baby's breast milk intake is to weigh a baby (naked) on a scale that measures pounds and ounces (kilograms and grams) before a feed and weigh them again after a feed. Some parents have done this with a home scale, whereas one will weigh themselves alone, then weigh themselves again while holding their naked baby, and then repeat this weighing method after a feed. Do this several times a day for two to three days to determine the baby's average intake. This will help you determine your breast milk production.

Breastfeeding Essentials

Size of a newborn's stomach

Day 1	**Day 3**	**Day Week**	**One Month**
size of a cherry	size of a walnut	size of an apricot	size of a large egg
5 - 7 ml	22 - 27 ml	45 - 60 ml	80 - 150 ml
1 - 1.4 tablespoons	0.75 -1oz	1.5 - 2 oz	2.5 - 5 oz

Health & Parenting

I have also witnessed petite families with petite babies challenged greatly about their baby's being underweight. In this situation, as a consultant I perform a thorough oral exam, latch evaluation and pre and post feed weight check, as I do with all consults. If all proves normal, then I put my midwifery hat on and evaluate the baby's developmental milestones depending on their age. Ultimately, as a mother you can see when something is wrong with a baby. Likewise, you can also see when a baby is thriving. In most of these cases the petite baby has proven to be thriving normally.

A baby who gains weight naturally will display specific consistencies such as:

- Reach birth weight within 10 – 14 days postpartum.
- A certain growth curve for weight, length, and head circumference.
- Wakes independently to breastfeed about 8 to 12 times in 24 hours.

- Meets expected number of soiled diapers daily.

On the contrary genuine low birth weight or slow weight-gain babies:

- Usually do not reach their birth weight within two weeks postpartum.
- Disproportionate growth curve for weight, length, and head circumference.
- May cry inconsolably during a feed or immediately after.
- May reject the breast.
- May be lethargic and show signs of dehydration.
- Have less than expected daily soiled diapers.

Oral Thrush

Thrush is caused by an overgrowth of the Candida fungus in the mouth. Candida lives all over our bodies and is given a different name depending on the location of the overgrowth. On the feet it is termed Athletes Foot; in the groin area it is called yeast infection or Jock Itch; on the scalp we call it dandruff or cradle cap (potentially caused by candida); and in the mouth, it is referred to as thrush.

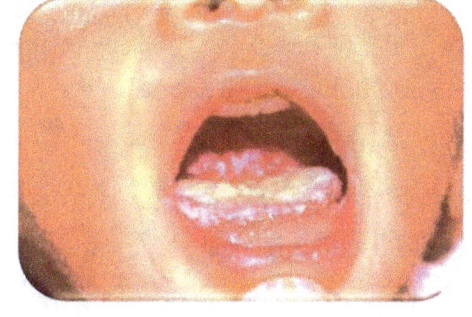

My first bout with thrush was while breastfeeding my eldest child. He was close to four months, and I believed he was teething for about two weeks.

Breastfeeding Essentials

He was drooling profusely and clearly irritated orally. He would take any toy, blanket, clothing, etc. and rub his mouth with it. Once my nipples began to itch and peel, I then knew something was wrong. Breastfeeding support in the 90's in the black community was scarce to none (especially within my family) and Dr. Google was not a "thing" yet, so I referenced books to learn what was causing my symptoms. Here is where I learned about thrush. The details were exact. My baby even had the small white patches on the inner lining of his cheeks and a white coated tongue.

Being a newfound naturalist, I was hesitant to give my baby antifungal drops or take any "quick-fix" pills. My only options were tea tree oil and gentian violet. Both are natural antifungals. I also dosed up on eating raw garlic. Several times daily, I would wipe my baby's mouth clean and my breasts with a diluted mixture of apple cider vinegar and water. Followed by a generous coating of gentian violet, both on my nipples and areola, and within his mouth. What you should know about gentian violet is that the name is derived from its deep purple color. Gentian violet, much like other beautiful bold colors from nature such as turmeric, indigo, and henna, has been traditionally used as a dye. So, as you can imagine, my boobs and my baby's mouth were stained violet for weeks! I perceived this as a mild inconvenience for an all-natural treatment. The herb is breastfeeding friendly, which made my baby's poop stain purple as well. This let me know that the gentian violet was working to alleviate the overgrowth of candida both superficially and internally. I am happy to say that we never had thrush again.

Practice • Patience • Persistence

Please note that my experience with thrush as a newfound naturalist worked for me at the time, I encourage all parents to do their own research before introducing any form of herbal or medicinal treatment to their babies. There are ample resources available now. Far more than I had access to while breastfeeding my first baby.

When a baby has oral thrush, some of the following associating symptoms may accompany:

- Drooling
- White patches on inner-cheeks and on tongue
- Diaper rash
- Crying while rubbing their mouth

Some associating symptoms in mom are:
- Itchy or burning nipples that appear pink or reddish, shiny, flaky, and/or have a rash with tiny blisters.
- The nipples can be cracked or blistered.
- Shooting pains in the breast during or after feedings
- Intense nipple or breast pain that is not improved with better latch-on and positioning.

Both mom and baby can share this yeast overgrowth and it can be difficult to determine which is the host. Therefore, it is best for both mom and baby to be treated simultaneously. The cause of thrush is rooted in sugar and moisture. As such it can easily be controlled by managing these two factors. The following tips can help to reduce candida growth and prevent recontamination:

Breastfeeding Essentials

- Avoid refined sugars, high carbohydrate foods and alcohol.
- Allow your breasts to air dry and avoid wearing breast pads during treatment; or only use disposable pads.
- Apply a diluted solution of tea tree oil and a carrier oil (coconut, grapeseed, jojoba, etc.) liberally on the nipples and areola daily during treatment.
- Cleanse and boil all applicable teething baby toys, pacifiers, and bottles nipples daily for 20 minutes.
- If you are pumping, boil all breast pump parts that are in contact with breast milk, and change the membranes.
- Pour rubbing alcohol through your pump tubing and allow it to air dry.
- Pre-soak cloth breast pads and diapers in a mixture of white vinegar and water.

Reoccurring thrush for either mom or baby should be taken seriously. Candida is a very opportunistic organism. It thrives in acidic environments. Familiarize yourself with alkaline foods to help change your body chemistry into one that is inhabitable for candida overgrowth and other harmful viruses and bacteria.

Mastitis

Mastitis is an inflammation of a mammary gland within the breast tissue. It is usually caused by a bacterial infection from a damaged nipple or a clogged milk duct. Similar to leaving a milk substance on the counter of your home for a few days, eventually the milk would be overcome with bacteria and spoil. When milk is left trapped in a gland then it can spoil and become infected.

Once this happens the body reacts with flu-like symptoms. Fever, chills, achy muscles, etc. The area surrounding the affected gland becomes swollen with fluid as the body attempts to quarantine the infection. Hence mastitis commonly appears as a hard, isolated mass within the breast that is unusually warm and tender to pressure.

The cause of mastitis is rooted in restricted milk flow. This is why engorged breasts are vulnerable to mastitis. The glands become overfull and may not all release during one feeding or pumping. Tight bras or underwire in bras can also be restrictive to milk flow, specifically to the glands underneath the breasts and within the armpits. Routine breasts massage either during a feeding or after can help prevent mastitis.

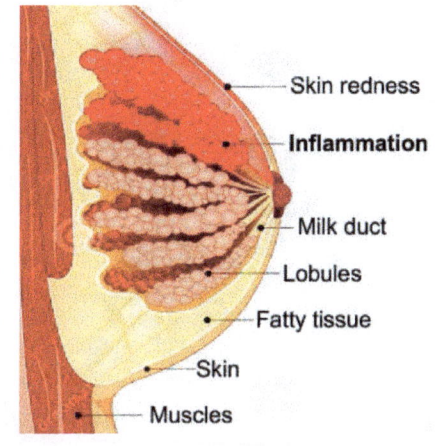

This infection can range from mild to severe. I was fortunate to only have mastitis once and it was a mild case. I was advised by my elders to "take the baby to bed." They did not know what it was, they could only see that I was not feeling well. My treatment was intentional resting, increased water/fluids, vitamin C and Echinacea herbal tea for about 48 hours. I intuitively breastfed more frequently on the unknowingly infected breast because it felt relieved each time. As my baby nursed, I would apply gentle pressure to the affected area, again for relief. I later learned of mastitis and knew immediately from the described associated symptoms that I had experienced this infection.

I give thanks that I had a supportive family and the ability to listen to my body. Many women with mastitis are treated with antibiotics and discouraged from breastfeeding. They are recommended to pump and dump. These providers are unaware that most antibiotics taken by mom are safe for breastfeeding. Thankfully, families can research medications online now to find up-to-date information about the interactions of specific prescription medications and breast milk.

Practice • Patience • Persistence

Dispelling 19 Myths About Breastfeeding

1. My breasts are too small.

This is a common misconception attached to women with smaller breast cup sizes. I was told this by several family members when I decided to breastfeed my first child. They believed that because I was an A cup before pregnancy, that I would not produce an adequate milk supply to sustain my baby. I honestly do not recall if their doubt discouraged me. Fortunately, at that time of my life I was coming into my awakening of self-discovery and right knowledge. My belief system was being weeded out and replaced with science and facts. This made me a more independent thinker. I knew that if I could co-create a child then my body could certainly make the milk....and it did! As expected, I produced more milk than necessary within the first days postpartum.

In chapter 3, *What is Milk*, the milk production process is explained. Breast tissue, glands, ducts, etc., grow or mature in order to produce milk. Women who began pregnancy with an A or B cup, may find themselves wearing a C or D cup by mid-pregnancy. Some of these women will return to their pre-pregnancy cup size after weaning; many will not.

2. Large breasts make more milk.

This is not true! The cup size does not dictate the amount of milk that a woman will produce. I have witnessed A cups become over-producers just as often as DD cups. On the contrary, I have witnessed DD cups challenged with low milk supply as well.

Ultimately, about 10-14 days postpartum, a mother's breast will produce milk based on her output or stimulation. This process is explained in more detail in chapter 3.

3. My nipples are too flat.

Flat nipples can prove to be problematic for breastfeeding. The reason is due to a baby's sucking reflex, located about one inch deep at the roof of their mouths. Once the baby latches and begins to suck, this reflex must be repeatedly stimulated to encourage the baby to continue to suck. When this reflex is not stimulated, then the baby will release their latch in frustration.

There are several breastfeeding support items to aid in this dilemma. All of them are designed to attempt to pull the nipple more forward. Using a breast pump prior to a feed can also prove beneficial for achieving this goal. The pump will help the nipple to erect and protrude more, providing more surface area for the baby to latch on. Having a partner to suck at your nipples, vigorously, prior to a feed can help achieve this same goal.

If your efforts to latch with flat nipples begin to feel futile, then take a break and pump. Give your baby your breast milk via a syringe, spoon, medicine dropper or use the paced bottle-feeding technique (detailed in chapter 6). Frustration and aggravation only upsets baby and makes breastfeeding become a dreadful experience. Remember that your postpartum hormones are unstable, and it is common to feel emotional. My lactation mentor, Theresa Byrd, taught us to always, "feed the baby; then fix the problem."

If at first you don't succeed, try & try again!

It is okay if you need to pump or hand express breast milk for a few days while you learn to latch your baby. We want baby and mommy to feel rewarded during a nursing session. Babies are surprisingly adaptable.

They are hard-wired to breastfeed. I believe mothers are as well. This is why co-sleeping skin-to-skin (on a firm mattress with minimum pillows) can be helpful for encouraging breastfeeding. During those mid-awake moments, our primitive brains can control the feed without us overthinking the process. Though, if problems persist, it is also beneficial to seek out support from a lactation counselor.

4. My nipples are too large.

Most breastfeeding mother's nipples fit perfectly within their baby's oral cavity. Rarely will nipples prove to be too large for a baby's mouth, but it does happen. I have only witnessed this about four times out of hundreds of women. During these rare occasions, the baby was able to latch and suckle to satisfaction. Unfortunately, the mom was in excruciating pain because her nipples were very large (about the diameter of a quarter), the baby was only able to latch onto her nipple and not much of the areola. Nipple feeding is painful!

Sadly, I was not able to assist these women with successful latching. My best advice was to continue pumping over the next few weeks. Feed the baby with a cup, syringe, spoon, or paced bottle feeding. Maintain finger suckling to help baby remember to latch on skin, and periodically attempt to latch baby as their mouth's grow. Eventually, the baby's oral cavity will catch up to the mother's nipple.

5. I can't have alcohol while breastfeeding.

This is a complete myth. The most important concept to remember when consuming alcohol while breastfeeding is that everyone has an individual alcohol tolerance level. A safe rule to follow for alcohol consumption while breastfeeding is, "if you are sober enough to drive, then you are okay to breastfeed".

As mentioned in chapter 5, alcohol is a dehydrant and can interfere with milk production because breast milk requires water for production Alcohol also easily transfuses in and out of breast milk. As the mother sobers, the alcohol returns to her blood supply for elimination. It is best to eliminate alcohol through the urine instead of pumping and dumping which can actually cause more alcohol to infuse into the breast milk. However, it is also a good idea to pump in small amounts in effort to prevent engorgement. More information on this subject can be found in chapter 5.

6. I can't smoke cigarettes while breastfeeding.

Smoking and breastfeeding can be a very controversial topic. Even more so than drinking alcohol while breastfeeding. When used long-term, both can cause harm to mom and baby and should be avoided while breastfeeding. However, though smoking cigarettes and cigars is strongly discouraged while nursing, science and evidence supports that this mother's milk is still better for her baby than formula.

As reviewed in chapter 5, the key here is eliminating second-hand smoke which is even more detrimental than the trace nicotine found in breast milk.

Smoking of any kind is not recommended during breastfeeding. Nicotine does impact breast milk supply and in small amounts it will leech into the breast milk. The second-hand smoke either in the air or the smoke that remains on the clothes and skin is more harmful to baby than the amount found in the breast milk. It has been determined that a woman who smokes 15-20 cigarettes daily is still safe to breastfeed her baby. Unfortunately, the nicotine tends to dehydrate whereby decreasing the milk supply.

If you are a smoker, be certain to always smoke outside away from your baby. Cover your hair and wear a designated robe or jacket while smoking. Be certain to remove these garments and wash your hands and face thoroughly after smoking and before engaging your baby. And always smoke after a feed, not before.

7. I must eat healthy while breastfeeding.

On average, people tend to have more concern about their eating habits while breastfeeding than while pregnant. Pregnancy has this stigma of *eating for two* which unfortunately grants opportunity for women to overindulge in food -- poor quality foods in many cases, and then suffer pregnancy induced illnesses like gestational diabetes or hypertension (high blood pressure). In fact, pregnancy is a critical time to select high quality foods because everything the mother consumes is directly affecting the growth and development of her baby. Breast milk, on the contrary, is initiated by fat and fluid reserves within the body. Breast milk is highly resilient to a mother's eating habits and, in most cases, will persist to produce sufficient amounts even on food rations such as diets composed primarily of grains (rice, millet, corn or sorghum) and small amounts of vegetables or occasional meat.

Some research reveals that breastfeeding requires more calories than pregnancy to sustain milk production – about 200 more. However, it is strongly recommended that a woman allows her appetite to be her guide. There will be periods when your body will demand more calories and you will feel hungrier. This is typically during a growth spurt for your baby, and they are demanding more milk from you.

I encourage moms to continue with their prenatal vitamins and monitor their fluid intake while breastfeeding. Breast milk averages about 70-80% water, so it requires water for production. Also eat high quality foods for your personal health. When we consume crappy, low vibrational foods then we also feel crappy. So, consume live, fresh foods with vibrant colors and lots of green, not just in pregnancy or while breastfeeding but throughout life. You are what you eat!

8. I must wean if I am taking medication.

Many physicians will discourage women from breastfeeding while consuming any prescription medication without full knowledge of any contraindications. Most medications like antibiotics, allergy, and blood pressure meds are breastfeeding friendly. There are several websites and other publications that commit to identifying safe usage of medications while breastfeeding.

In Chapter 5, I mentioned the LactMed® database. It provides an *updated database of drugs and dietary supplements that may affect breastfeeding*. It is a part of the National Library of Medicine's Toxicology Data Network.

9. I can't breastfeed while pregnant.

Breastfeeding while pregnant is perfectly safe so long as the mother is not feeling any uterine cramping sensations while nursing. This is an individual process that is primarily determined by comfort. Some women are comfortable breastfeeding throughout the entire pregnancy and will do so while continuing to tandem nurse postpartum. Others will wean during the pregnancy if the latching sensation becomes uncomfortable, then continue to tandem nurse postpartum. Then there are those like me who will wean the child permanently during the pregnancy.

10. I can't get pregnant while breastfeeding.

Yes, a woman can conceive while breastfeeding. Exclusive breastfeeding can suppress a woman's ovulation cycle and cause amenorrhea, no menstruation. Which is why exclusive breastfeeding can help with natural child spacing (1.5-2 years apart). However, this method of birth control can be unpredictable and is not 100% reliable if you are certain that you are not ready to conceive again. Because the cycle has been disrupted it can be difficult to identify when your body has begun to ovulate again, leaving opportunity for unexpected conception.

Breastfeeding in conjunction to condoms or diaphragms can be helpful. There is some research that reveals consumption of large quantities of Vitamin C (3000mg) for 2-3 days after sex can prevent untimely pregnancies. More details about birth control and breastfeeding can be found in chapter 5, **The Do's & Don'ts of Breastfeeding**

11. I can't breastfeed with a sexually transmitted infection, STI.

Most sexually transmitted infections (STI) such as chlamydia, syphilis, and gonorrhea do not transmit to baby while breastfeeding. In fact, as the mother's body is producing natural antibiotics to fight the infection, she will share those nature-induced immunities with her baby. Be certain to research the prescribed treatment or medications to be certain of any breast milk contradictions.

Genital herpes or Herpes Simplex Virus type 2 is only an issue if a lesion appears on the nipple. This lesion is considered to be infected and in direct contact it can transmit to baby. The mother can pump from the breast with the infected nipple and only nurse from the other non-infected nipple. Knowing that breast milk has abundance of natural antibacterial, antiviral, and antifungal properties, dumping the pumped milk becomes controversial. It is however recommended that the pump milk from the infected nipple be discarded.

HIV, human immunodeficiency virus, does have a probability of transferring to the baby through breast milk – even though a baby can be born HIV negative from an HIV positive mother. The United States Center for Disease Control advises for an HIV positive mother to abstain from breastfeeding regardless of her baby's HIV status.

Breastfeeding Essentials

Center for Disease Control and Prevention
The best way to prevent transmission of HIV to an infant through breast milk is to not breastfeed. In the United States, where mothers have access to clean water and affordable replacement feeding (infant formula), CDC and the American Academy of Pediatrics External recommend that HIV-infected mothers completely avoid breastfeeding their infants, regardless of ART [antiretroviral therapy] maternal viral load.

On the contrary the World Health Organization recommends that Breast is always best, even for HIV-positive mothers. They suggest that an HIV mother should indeed breastfeed her baby to help build the baby's lymphatic system (immune system) and reduce the risks of HIV.

World Health Organization
...WHO is recommending that HIV-positive mothers or their infants take antiretroviral drugs throughout the period of breastfeeding and until the infant is 12 months old. This means that the child can benefit from breastfeeding with very little risk of becoming infected with HIV.

12. I should never breastfeed someone else's baby.

Wet-Nursing, or breastfeeding someone else's baby, has become very taboo in the United States. Many women suffer embarrassment and ridicule for simply breastfeeding their own baby, let alone someone else's. It is more acceptable to milk share via pumping than to actually latch another woman's baby to your breasts. Milk sharing is also discouraged unless conducted through a reputable third-party distribution center.

I personally disagree! Wet-nursing was once, and still is in some communities, very common among the women. Remember that bottles and breast pumps are very new inventions in relation to hueman existence on this planet. Wet-nursing was considered convenient, helpful, and an act of bonding within tribes. Wet-nursing allowed babies to bond within the tribe to multiple moms and it also allowed the mothers to have nursing breaks. We can still see this behavior among other communal mammals such as felines, canine, bovine, apes, monkeys, and other mammalian animals.

Breast milk contains more than just water and nutrients – it also contains genetic material such as DNA, RNA, and a host of other subtle properties that we have yet to understand.

> US National Library of Medicine National Institutes of Health Search database
> ....Epithelial cells, which contain both RNA and DNA, make up 50-90% of cell types found in human breastmilk.

So, before you agree to allow another mom to breastfeed your baby be mindful of her-story in terms of health (mental and physical) and diseases. Be mindful that, though wet-nursing in most cases is safe, you should be fully aware of the mother's HIV and other STI status. You should also know if the mother is consuming any medications or other recreational drug use.

13. Formula is science and better than breast milk.

This is a complete fallacy! Modern European science is still in its infancy compared to hueman evolution. Breast milk is a synergistic part of life and necessary for continued survival. For this reason, it is organic (living, animated, biological) in its makeup and highly adaptable. Breast milk/mammalian milk is uniquely designed for the individual off-spring for each stage of development. Meaning it adapts and morphs to meet the needs of a newborn, infant, toddler, and two-year old.

Infant baby formula on the contrary is non-organic and it is always the same processed blend of ingredients each time it is prepared. The designer/scientist/nutritionist can change the recipe in effort to give breast milk qualities to the formula, however the final product continues to be synthetic and non-organic (living) with very few antibiotic properties. See chapter 3.

14. I can't breastfeed with breast implants.

Breast augmentation or implants, depending on the procedure, can impede breast milk production. Most implants within recent decades have been inserted behind the breast muscle which leaves the milk ducts and glands intact. This procedure typically does not interfere with breast milk production and mothers are able to achieve successful latching and nursing.

Implants that require the nipples to be removed for insertion usually sever the interior milk ducts and glands which can interfere with production. This is a special case which requires observation. Some of these women are able to achieve exclusive breastfeeding.

15. I had a breast reduction so I can't breastfeed.

A breast reduction can impede breast milk production depending on the procedure. In recent decades, when breast reduction surgery is performed on younger women there is consideration to preserving her milk ducts and glands. The surgeon attempts to remove fat tissue from around the ducts and glands to minimize any milk production complications.

This is a special case which requires observation. Some of these women are able to achieve exclusive breastfeeding.

16. My mom didn't make enough milk, so I probably won't either.

Anthropology is the study of hueman behavior, and it teaches us that huemans learn greatly through observing other huemans. For this reason, it is normal to *want* to adopt your mother's birth and breastfeeding story. This standard cannot be fully applied to our westernized society as it relates to birth and breastfeeding because there are far too many interventions and variables to consider. Nonetheless, your breastfeeding journey will be unique for both you and your baby(s). <u>If your mother experienced issues with breastfeeding this should not have any influence over your experience.</u> Many women born in the 1900's did not have appropriate information nor support for their breastfeeding efforts. Infant formula was the new "best" thing, and women were greatly discouraged from breastfeeding. It has only been within recent decades that women are returning to breastfeeding in greater numbers.

17. Colostrum is bad for the baby.

This is a complete myth and belief system carried by some indigenous and religious communities. I am not certain where this idea stemmed from, but it remains prevalent to this day. I have witnessed said communities hand express the colostrum and discard it. They will not latch the baby until the mature milk begins to develop about three days after birth. In between time they will either allow another mom to breastfeed the baby or feed the baby formula.

Colostrum is the first stage of breast milk production and critically important to the gut health of the baby. It is nutrient dense and abundant in antibiotics. It is essentially the first hueman food and helps to prepare the infant's gut for mature milk. See chapter 3.

18. My baby likes the bottle more than my breasts.

This is a misconception that parents can have after introducing the baby to an infant bottle and now the baby is appearing to reject the breast. Babies do not know how to breastfeed at birth. It is a learned behavior that requires muscle memory and builds cognition over time. When an artificial nipple is introduced before the baby has fully learned the art of breastfeeding then there is risk of disorienting their latching mechanics. See chapter 6, section *No Artificial Nipples for First Month*.

19. My baby likes the taste of formula more than my milk.

This is another misconception that parents can have after introducing the baby to an infant bottle and now the baby is appearing to reject the breast. Test trials have proven time after time that infants prefer their mother's milk over infant formula. You can do your own test at home. Pour some freshly expressed breast milk onto a clean unscented cloth. Then pour some freshly prepared formula onto a separate clean unscented cloth. Lay your baby down face up and place a cloth on either side of baby's ears. Watch which cloth your baby will gravitate towards. You can also perform

Practice • Patience • Persistence

this test with someone holding the baby and another person holding the cloths on either side of the baby. This test is best preformed while baby is quiet and content.

Breast milk allows your baby to taste a variety of different foods. It can have hints of flavors from the foods that the mother consumes. This encourages the child to eat more food variety during the formative years. See chapter 5.

Food for Thought

When to add solid foods

This can be a controversial topic. Even during my research, I was surprised to see that the American Academy of Pediatrics (AAP) presented vague information regarding when to introduce a baby to solid foods. Although, the website is specific about delaying the introduction of solids if the baby is formula fed.

> *American Academy of Pediatrics*
> *Formula fed infants are at more risk for early introduction of solids. Introduction to solids prior to 4 months is associated with increased weight gain and adiposity, both in infancy and early childhood.*

This is very contrary to what many families do for their formula-fed babies, which presents a strong correlation to the current childhood diabetes epidemic within the United States. Many of families will introduce their newborn to infant cereal and commercial baby food as early as one week postpartum. While I was working for WIC, a special supplemental nutrition program for Women, Infants, and Children, I witnessed families routinely mixing these items in with the infant formula to encourage the baby to sleep longer.

In short, there is not a timeline to determine when to introduce your baby to solid foods. Instead, we must give attention to the child's physiological maturity. There are three observable signs that determines when a growing baby's digestive system has developed adequately to receive foods other than breast milk.

Breastfeeding Essentials

1. The baby will begin to sit upright or make assertive efforts to sit upright. This reflects the nerves and spinal development which are necessary for proper digestion of solid food.
2. The baby will begin to use their pincer grasp reflexes which is the coordination of their index finger and their thumb to hold an item. This function allows the child to pick up small objects and bring it to their mouths.
3. The tongue thrust reflex descends deeper inside the baby's mouth. Meaning when a baby's lips are touched, their tongue will extend out of their mouth which allows for breast or bottle feeding but not spoon or cup feeding. As the child develops, this reflex has to be triggered further back into their mouths which then allows them to receive food from a spoon or cup.

It is best to wait until these signs are observed prior to feeding your baby solid foods. This can greatly help to avoid upsetting their digestive system and causing constipation or diarrhea.

Practice • Patience • Persistence

Closing Remind-hers

Vaccines and Breastfeeding

Childhood vaccinations have become a serious topic of discussion in recent years. I have seen families at odds about vaccinating their child. If there are strong opposing views about whether or not to vaccinate the child, then those families will typically compromise on a modified schedule and determine when they want to have the drug administered to their child.

The vaccine controversy has grown in light of the rapid and constant increase of children developing Autism, paralysis, and in some cases, death. There is an abundance of data, evidence, and research regarding vaccinations available to the public in all forms of media. There are families that attest without doubt that specific vaccinations caused injury to their child; likewise, there are scientist, physicians and other professionals that claim otherwise. The debate is strong, and the opposing views are intense. Is it a government conspiracy or paranoid parents? Are the physicians neglectful or are the scientist corrupt? Questions and concerns that create a big rabbit hole with no end.

I accept that truth is simple. Truth is always easy to grasp but, in some cases, difficult to face. Let us first accept that huemans, like every other species in nature, are born with immunizing capabilities. Yes, babies are born with underdeveloped lymphatic/immune systems, however a mother's body provides a variation of inoculant responses to initiate her baby's natural defenses. Beginning with a vaginal delivery which is the baby's first introduction to millions of bacteria that cover their little body's and triggers their microbiome to begin colonizing. This protective coating is then reinforced by skin-to-skin contact with both mom and dad. As the newborn baby licks and suckles at the mother's breasts and skin tissue, they swallow millions of bacteria that aid in cultivating their gut flora, which is reinforced at every feed and balanced by the mother's colostrum and soon after, her mature milk. This is natural immunization!

Vaccination is un-natural, and we must remember that unnatural behavior carries unnatural consequences – regardless of the intentions. Side-effects are the risks associated from in-taking man-made vaccines — an unnatural process. Just as there are risks associated with not breastfeeding and using man-made infant formula. In knowing this then it is of vital importance that the parent(s) be intensely responsible (response-able) to investigate any vaccine thoroughly prior to allowing their baby to be injected with it. We must be accountable for the choices that we make. It is far better to reach a comfortable, informed decision rather than a vulnerable, influenced decision. The latter has the potential for regret.

I cannot make light of this decision. It was a struggle for me and my was-bands. We decided against vaccinations for our children and this choice came with great adversity, primarily from family who feared our decision would bring harm to our children. This choice also came with some social isolation from lack of knowledge about disease transference. I believe for me the most challenging effect of our choice was the "normal" encounters with childhood illnesses. I was stressed with every cold, flu, or upset stomach. Again, this was due to a lack of knowledge and resources 20+ years ago. Nowadays, with the internet and social media, families can find like-mined groups and an abundance of information to help alleviate the fears that we were challenged with. Youth of today can lean into one-another for support and advise when you have concerns about your non-vaccinated baby's symptoms. There are also pediatricians that support non-vaccination and are willing to share their expertise.

Regardless of whether you opt for complete vaccination, partial vaccination, or decide against it altogether, the crucial aspect is that your decision is based on accurate information, and you find peace with the consequences of your choice.

About the author

Sekesa Berry is a Birth Justice Activist and community leader for Black Birth Workers. She honors many titles such as the Founder and Executive Director of the Atlanta Doula Collective, Inc. non-profit organization, Developer of the Maternal Health Consultant Training (MHC), a.k.a. Advanced Doula Skills Training, a Lactation Consultant, a Community Midwife and now Author. The title that Sekesa holds above all others is Mother. She is a loving mother of four children and a community mother to many.

Sekesa is one of Georgia's most knowledgeable and active community leaders for Black maternal health and the Birth Justice movement. As an advocate of reproductive justice, Sekesa has worked closely with several organizations and local non-profit foundations in an effort to decolonize birth, curtail birth traumas, and restore natural birth rights to Black families. For nearly two decades, she has dedicated herself to a multitude of roles and strengthened her skills and knowledge in perinatal support. Her maternal health work experience includes, namely: Women Infant Children Program as a Breastfeeding Counselor; Bellies-To-Babies Foundation as a Program Manager; SisterSong Women of Color

Practice • Patience • Persistence

Reproductive Justice Collective, as a Birth Justice Consultant; and Black Mothers Matter Alliance as a Kindred Partner.

Sekesa has extensive experience supporting families with breastfeeding. She was initiated into the lactation profession by her personal experiences with breastfeeding her four children well into toddlerhood. Her lactation support skills were further cultivated when she began helping families as a Labor Support Specialist (doula) in 2006. Sekesa was later offered a job as a WIC Breastfeeding Peer Counselor in 2010, while visiting a WIC office to pick up vouchers for her family. This foundation helped to set a model for hands-off breastfeeding support that was centered in counseling — not touching. Sekesa quickly learned the importance of encouraging a mother to self-latch her baby in effort to influence long-term breastfeeding. Her work along with her passion for educating families about breastfeeding motivated Sekesa to continue her lactation education by becoming a Certified Lactation Counselor in 2012. Upon leaving WIC, Sekesa worked for several years as a Lactation Consultant in both obstetrical and independent Midwifery offices. To date as a Community Midwife, Sekesa has supported hundreds of families, both in-home and in-clinic, with breastfeeding issues. She truly believes that breastmilk is one of the best preventative superfoods that nature provides for all mammalian species.

Thank You!

Bibliography

"African American Health Disparities Compared to Non-Hispanic Whites." *Families Usa*, Jan. 2019, familiesusa.org/resources/african-american-health-disparities-compared-to-non-hispanic-whites/.

Ballard, Olivia, and Ardythe L Morrow. "Human milk composition: nutrients and bioactive factors." *Pediatric clinics of North America* vol. 60,1 (2013): 49-74. doi:10.1016/j.pcl.2012.10.002

Baumgartel, Kelley L, and Yvette P Conley. "The utility of breastmilk for genetic or genomic studies: a systematic review." *Breastfeeding medicine: the official journal of the Academy of Breastfeeding Medicine* vol. 8,3 (2013): 249-56. doi:10.1089/bfm.2012.0054

"Breast Is Always Best, Even for HIV-Positive Mothers." *World Health Organization*, World Health Organization, 4 Mar. 2011, www.who.int/bulletin/volumes/88/1/10-030110/en/.

Cassella, Carly. "No One Is Talking About The Environmental Impacts of The Baby Formula Industry." *ScienceAlert*, 2018, www.sciencealert.com/no-one-is-talking-about-the-environmental-impacts-of-the-baby-formula-industry.

Dadhich, JP, et al. "Carbon Footprints Due to Milk Formula. A Study from Selected Countries of the Asia Pacific Region." *ResearchGate*, Breastfeeding Promotion Network of India/International Baby Food Action Network, 2015, www.researchgate.net/publication/301289819_Carbon_Foot prints_Due_to_Milk_Formula_A_study_from_selected_count ries_of_the_Asia_Pacific_region.

D. Hileti-Telfer. *Encyclopedia of Food Sciences and Nutrition.* 2nd ed., Elsevier Science Ltd, 2003.

Heyman, Melvin B and Committee on Nutrition. "Lactose Intolerance in Infants, Children, and Adolescents." *American Academy of Pediatrics*, American Academy of Pediatrics, 1 Sept. 2006, pediatrics.aappublications.org/content/118/3/1279.

Hopper, Jessica. "Formula for Theft Success: Steal Food For a Baby." *Abcnews*, 4 April 2011, https://abcnews.go.com/US/baby-formula-targeted-organized-retail-theft-rings/story?id=13293485.

"Human Immunodeficiency Virus (HIV)." *Centers for Disease Control and Prevention*, Centers for Disease Control and Prevention, 4 Feb. 2020, www.cdc.gov/breastfeeding/breastfeeding-special-circumstances/maternal-or-infant-illnesses/hiv.html.

"Infant Food and Feeding." *AAP.org*, American Academy of Pediatrics, 2020, www.aap.org/en-us/advocacy-and-policy/aap-health-initiatives/HALF-Implementation-Guide/Age-Specific-Content/Pages/Infant-Food-and-Feeding.aspx.

Niala, JC. "Why African Babies Don't Cry." *InCultureParent*, https://www.incultureparent.com/why-african-babies-dont-cry/

Nixon, Robin. "Breast Milk Does DNA Good." *LiveScience*, Purch, 2010, www.livescience.com/6498-breast-milk-dna-good.html.

Happe, Randolph, and Luisa Gambelli. "Infant Formula." *Food Science, Technology and Nutrition*, 2015, 285-315.

"Smoking & Breastfeeding." *La Leche League GB*, La Leche League GB, 10 Mar. 2016, www.laleche.org.uk/smoking-breastfeeding/.

"Special Supplemental Nutrition Program for Women, Infants, and Children (WIC)." *USDA*, U.S. Department of Agriculture, 2020, www.fns.usda.gov/wic.

Stone, Ray. *The Best Damn Prostate Book*. Ra One Publications, 2019.

The Children's Hospital of Philadelphia. "Babies Fed Soy-Based Formula Have Changes in Reproductive System Tissues." *Children's Hospital of Philadelphia*, The Children's Hospital of Philadelphia, 12 Mar. 2018, www.chop.edu/news/babies-fed-soy-based-formula-have-changes-reproductive-system-tissues.

www.ingramcontent.com/pod-product-compliance
Lightning Source LLC
Chambersburg PA
CBHW070502090426
42735CB00012B/2655